<u>ReFire</u>ment™

A Boomer's Guide to Life After 50

ReFirement™

A Boomer's Guide to Life After 50

James V. Gambone, Ph.D.

Kirk House Publishers
Minneapolis, Minnesota

Refirement
A Boomer's Guide to Life After 50

ReFirement™ is a registered trademark of Points Of View Incorporated.
www.pointsofviewinc.com

Designed for the aging eye by Elder Eye Design,
Cover design concept by Steven Trofka

10   9   8   7   6   5   4   3   2   1

Library of Congress Cataloging-in-Publication Data
Gambone, James V.
    Refirement: A boomer's guide to life after 50 / by James V. Gambone
        p. cm.
    ISBN 1-886513-26-0 (alk. paper) -- ISBN 1-886513-25-2
        1. Retirment--United States--Psychoogical aspects. 2. Baby boom
    geration--United States--Psychology. I. Title
    HQ1063.2.U6 G35 2000
    306.3'8'0973--dc21
                                                            00-063329

Kirk House Publishers, PO Box 309459, Minneapolis, MN 55439
www.kirkhouse.com
Manufactured in the United States of America.

I dedicate this book to my wife and partner in life, Wendy Johnson. Her own dedication to creativity, learning, and caring for all of nature's creatures is an ongoing reminder of what ReFirement can mean in my life. Her loving eye watched over the content and design of this book. Her support and encouragement helped make it a reality.

Acknowledgments

There are so many people I want to acknowledge and thank. This book was a collaborative process involving all generations and people from all walks of life. Collaborators included: readers, professional writers, editors, specific content experts, and friends. Some shared their stories with me and gave me permission to use them in this book. And some I will probably miss on this page but their absence is not intentional.

I would like to thank **Jean Trumbauer.** She believed in this book and in ReFirement from the start and helped me frame much of the early outline. She acted as a supportive but critical editor during the early writing. Her sensitivity and expertise on women's issues and spirituality added a perspective and information base I could not have otherwise brought to this work. She is listed in the People and Other Resources section at the end of the book.

Ann Bauleke is a professional writer who also helped me at the beginning of this effort by showing me the power of writing from my heart and soul. She was an important inspiration.

Ron Klug, my editor, was a joy to work with. Ron helped me see the organization of the book in a fresh way, and reordered the book with a much improved structure from my original. He was diligent, sensitive, and supportive. Ron was there for me whenever I needed him. He is a "pro" in every sense of the word.

My list of readers included: **Ted Bowman, Jean Trumbauer, John Sippola, Judy Carlson, Helene Dudley, Donald Schmitz, Diane Shalue, Richard Morgan, Judy McVean, Steve Shank, Elizabeth Higginbotham, Wendy Johnson, Susan Foster** (who also helped prepare the original book proposal), **Joe Garbarino, Sue Gehrz, Peter Bailey, Gerry Richman,** and **Janet Fleming.** These people gave me their time, their considered opinions, and their unflinching support.

I am very grateful to my "ReFirement Pioneers": **Emily Kimball, Richard Morgan, Vilma Vitanza, Jim Rodgers** (whose story unfortunately did not make the final cut but was very important to me), and **Fred Ramstedt.** Each of these individuals went against the grain of their own generations and each is leading a rich and meaningful ReFired life.

Content experts included:

David Morgan, professor of Sociology and Urban Planning at Portland State University and editor of the *Generations Journal* issue, "The Baby Boom at Midlife and Beyond."

Peter Radcliff, professor of History at Macalaster College in St. Paul. Peter introduced me to a variety of resources on poor and working class values.

Lillian Rubin, who has written extensively on demythologizing working class values and the pains of coming from a working class background.

Barbara Jensen, a therapist and professor at Metropolitan State University, who has written most extensively on what it means to be a professional coming from working class roots.

Elizabeth Higginbotham, a professor at the University of Delaware, who has written extensively on the differences in mobility experienced by African American women coming from poor, working, and middle class backgrounds.

Peg Wetli, the founder of the largest educational children theater company in the U.S. (CLIMB Theatre). Peg spends one extended lunch time with me each month talking about creative ideas and, by example, encouraging me to seek more creativity in my life.

Kayellen Taylor, a gem of a research librarian at the University of Minnesota. She is also a Boomer who wants to ReFire as an artist. She gave me a great assist with academic data bases and search engines.

Tom O'Connell, a professor of Labor History and Studies at Metropolitan State University in St. Paul. Tom connected me to Barbara Jensen and Lillian Rubin.

Jim Barrett, the chair of the History Department at University of Illinois in Urbana. Jim and I had conversations about what it means to have a Ph.D. yet come from a working class background.

Ted Bowman, who helped me understand the importance of what happens when you lose your dreams and how to create new ones.

Phil Styrlund, a corporate vice president but really a philosopher and friend who has challenged me with new ideas and ways to look at the world.

And last, but certainly not least, my wife **Wendy Johnson,** who lived with this book from its initial inception and rode through the ups and downs of agents, publishers, rejection letters, television deals, writer's blocks, and other minor depressions of the author. She has acted as an editor, a critic, a supporter, and most important, someone who believes in me and the potential of ReFirement.

Contents

Introduction

Why ReFirement?

Helene served with me as a volunteer in the Peace Corps in 1968. After the Peace Corps, she married, raised five children, and worked in the public sector of a major Southern urban county. Helene was directly in charge of billing and collecting $100 million annually in solid waste fees. The system she managed was heavily dependent on computer interfaces linking the Solid Waste Department with the Building and Zoning, Tax Collection, and Tax Assessor files. As the manager of Revenue Collections, she had three fulltime data-processing staff assigned to provide computer support.

Like others in public sector positions, Helene was forced to take on more responsibilities with less staff support. For an honest, professional, dedicated public servant, she found the politics of this particular county government hard to accept. But the pay was good and steady, the benefits outstanding, and Helene was getting close to retiring with a comfortable pension.

She noticed she was getting less and less fulfillment out of her work. Helene didn't want to wait until the job sapped more of her vital energy. She eventually asked herself, "Do I want to spend eight hours a day, five days a week, forty-eight weeks a year for the next twelve to fourteen years doing what

I've been doing?" Helene decided she wanted more from life and she had some valuable skills to offer the world. She was ready to ReFire.

At the age of fifty-one, Helene quit her secure job and rejoined the Peace Corps. She worked in Slovakia for two years, helping that country build more democratic institutions. She was able to travel to Russia, the Czech Republic, Austria, Hungary, Poland, France, and Italy. She came back to the U.S. refreshed and ReFired. She is not sure about the future but is positive she made the right decision. She is working temporary professional jobs until a more permanent job becomes available with the Peace Corps or some other international volunteer agency.

Donald is a new friend fifty-four years old—on the oldest edge of the Baby Boomer cohort. After spending twenty years in elementary education, Donald went through his first ReFirement at the age of forty-two. He quit teaching to help his wife develop one of the most successful temporary-staffing agencies in the upper Midwest.

Despite all his business successes, he kept asking the question, "Is this all there is?"

After a time, he met a wonderful older mentor who helped him identify his real passion—grandparenting. He decided, based on his Boomer values and experiences, that his generation needed a new definition of what it means to be a grandparent in the twenty-first century. His dream is to create a Grandparents Camp where kids and their grandparents can spend quality time together, develop support groups on the web, work with outplacement programs of large corporations to teach the values of grandparenting, and become the leading source of education on grandparenting issues.

Don is also excited, renewed, dedicated, and just received a master's degree in Human Development. Don is ReFiring.

Helene and Donald are the cutting edge of a new and dynamic social movement and lifestyle change that I call ReFirement. It is a lifestyle especially suited for the seventy-six million men and women of my generation, the Baby Boomers, who were born near or immediately after the end of World War Two, (1945-1963). While I am writing this book especially for Baby Boomers, I believe generations on either side of Boomers will find the idea of ReFirement exciting, challenging, and life-enhancing.

ReFirement began as a very small idea in 1994. Roy Fairfield and I were discussing the state of education. After he secured his Ph.D. from Harvard, Roy's life and educational career was all about educational reform. He believed that many intelligent and capable adults were denied access to higher education because it did not value their work and life experiences as worthy of academic credit. Roy, along with others, created the concept of "University without Walls." Following this idea, working men and women were taught how to translate their life experiences into college credit. Their goal was to produce educational portfolios that would be recognized by universities, colleges, and community colleges. Millions of working men and women now have undergraduate and even graduate degrees because of people like Roy Fairfield.

At the time Roy and I were talking about our lives, our work, and our passions, Roy was in his early seventies. He told me about one of his current assignments, developing an interdisciplinary program for a start-up Internet company that was creating a virtual university on the Web. During our conversation Roy mentioned something about "refiring" in his older years. I interrupted, "Excuse me Roy, but don't you mean *retiring?*" He replied, "No, I said ReFiring!" He had long ago stopped using the word *retiring* because to him it literally meant to get tired twice!

The word "ReFiring" stuck in my mind. I've told the story about Roy and our conversation many times in speeches and workshops during the last six years, and it never ceases to make people first laugh and then pause to think about its implications. People of all ages tell me how nice it is to have a different word that gives a different meaning to retirement. The idea of ReFiring has been appealing to me. After all, my own changing life and career path has always required getting "fired up" in order to learn new things.

So I ask, why not build onto Roy's personal perspective of ReFirement and replace the word *retirement* completely? ReFiring and ReFirement can give us all a much larger vision for the future. ReFirement is a positive and optimistic vision of how to live a meaningful life. It has a beneficial impact on others as we grow older and leave a permanent legacy for future generations. Plus, it provides an exciting platform for Boomers facing the challenges and opportunities of midlife. ReFirement describes midlife changes in a more positive light than the currently espoused midlife terms such as

> *"ReFirement is a positive and optimistic vision of how to live a meaningful life."*

"retreading," "reinventing," or "redesigning." ReFirement can also address both political and personal issues. It recognizes that, for any substantive change to be truly meaningful and long lasting, it must start and be rooted in the hearts and minds of individual men and women.

There is no more appropriate symbol for this new paradigm of aging than "fire." To pass through fire is symbolic of transcending the human condition. The *Dictionary of Symbols* says that the ancient Chinese describe fire as connected to "life, health, and spiritual energy." The alchemists, who believed all things derive from and return to fire, called fire "transforming and regenerative." And early Christians connected fire with purification and victory over evil. The authors of *Myths, Dreams and Mysteries* say fire embraces good and bad, and "it implies the desire to annihilate time and bring all things to their end." You may recall that every celebration of the new millennium, broadcast on television worldwide, used fire as its focal symbol for beginning a new century.

ReFirement transcends the traditional model of retirement. As Boomers continue our journey of self-discovery as aging members of a high-tech society, we will look to our own values to help us transform and regenerate ourselves. Imagine seventy-six million Americans in their late fifties, sixties, seventies, eighties, and even nineties, who value a meaningful life more than material possessions and are totally engaged in their communities. Imagine them appreciating every human asset and skill people possess. In ReFirement people will not be forced to quit working or be financially penalized for working because of their age. (This has already begun to happen with the unanimous congressional repeal of the Social Security working penalty.)

ReFirement promises to promote a nation of energetic and compassionate elders dedicated to community service. Under the common banner of service, we will celebrate our growing racial, cultural, and ethnic diversity. Think of the political impact aging and ReFiring Boomers will have when they engage in an honest dialogue with all living generations. Boomers can use their ReFirement to set a light under their passion for purposes such as how to distribute both abundant and scarce resources to promote human dignity and ensure a better world for future generations. These are a few of the exciting promises of ReFirement.

The Benefits of ReFirement

I am very excited about the future. I have dedicated myself to promoting the benefits of ReFirement for all living generations. The ReFirement lifestyle outlined in this book will enable you to create a good life with these essential skills:

- Understanding yourself and your values (Chapter 1)
- Accepting your own aging (Chapter 2)
- Saying no to retirement (Chapter 3)
- Getting your groove back (Chapter 4)
- Taking charge of your health and balancing your life (Chapter 5)
- Exploring better ways to live with gender differences (Chapter 6)
- Healing the divisions in our society (Chapter 7)
- Recovering your idealism as an Elder-in-Training (Chapter 8)

- Energizing yourself through what spirits you (Chapter 9)

- Developing your "Individual ReFirement Plan" (Chapter 10)

- Claiming your legacy (Chapter 11)

- Networking with others to build a worldwide ReFirement movement (Chapter 12)

But before we begin to better understand ReFirement and its many benefits, we need to carefully look at ourselves as a generation. What are our values? What do we bring with us that will help or hinder our aging process? Who are we really?

Special note: This book is filled with **Activities to ReFire Your Life.**  They will help you build a solid, personal ReFirement foundation. In some chapters, the activities will come at the end of the chapter. In other chapters they will be interspersed with the main body of the text to give you a break in reading or to emphasize a particular point. I suggest that you get a notebook in which to write your responses to the exercises. It will become your personal ReFirement journal.

Activities to ReFire your life

Identifying Interesting Peers

Make a list of people of your own age who are living their lives differently from you. What are the differences between your life and theirs? What things do you admire about these people? What can you learn from these individuals that you would like to incorporate into your lifestyle?

Developing Long-Term Plans

Think about what you might be doing in fifteen or twenty years. Are there things you can be doing right now to help you prepare for a longer-term vision of your life? What can you do next week to get started on your ReFirement?

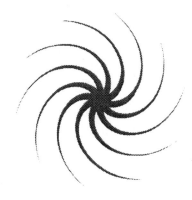

Chapter 1

Boomers – Who Are We Really?

Baby Boomers are the largest generation in American history. We number between seventy-six to eighty-four million people (depending on which year you believe the first or last Boomers were born and if you count immigrants). We make up nearly one-third of the United States population. And there are even more of us per capita in Canada! In the United States one Boomer turns fifty every eight seconds, and this will continue well into the future.

The sheer size of our group means that every characteristic of the generation has a greatly magnified impact on the entire culture. Some have likened us to a pig passing through the body of a python. From the day the first Boomer was born, everything in America has changed to accommodate us. We have experienced new schools, products, media, technology, roads, services, and subdivisions. It is no wonder we became hooked on their own importance and on the notion of change.

So who are we? In many ways we differ from one another. Some of us were hippies in urban communes or back-to-the-land settlements; others pursued MBAs. Some of us fought and died in Vietnam; others protested the war or fled to Canada. Some settled in suburbia and imitated the 1950s lifestyle of our parents; others stayed in the cities to gentrify poor neighborhoods and become the new urban landed gentry. But one thing most of us had in common: we were born into working class, poor, or small business families.

A Big Boomer Secret

Despite everything written about the Baby Boomers, one fact has been overlooked: Nearly seventy-five percent, or about fifty-seven million Baby Boomers, come from economically poor, working class, or small family-owned business roots.[1]

"Nearly 75 percent (of the) Baby Boomers, come from economically poor, working class, or small family-owned business roots."

There are two reasons why this information is particularly significant now. First, millions of aging professional or career-minded Baby Boomers who grew up in working class, poor, or small-entrepreneurial families struggle with the psychological effects of having crossed class lines. Secondly, there are important positive values many of us learned in our childhood and teen years that need to be reintegrated into the aging process of all seventy-six million Boomers.

Being disconnected or confused about one's personal history is neither comfortable nor healthy. So, it should come as no surprise that many Boomers feel as if they just don't quite fit in. "Awkward" might be the better word for a generation of young people who learned about the classics through Classic Comics, or saw their first professional theater, ballet, or symphony production when they went to

---

[1]See figure 1 in Chapter Notes, pg. 197.

college. Today, one of the hottest on-line discussions among Boomer academics from poor and working class backgrounds is how to reconcile their "lowbrow" backgrounds with their "highbrow" faculty positions.

Many of us also harbor lingering feelings of resentment and anger that our stories have never been properly told. (I am still waiting for the film or television special that talks about my life during the 1960s and '70s.) Most of the major institutions in our society are dominated by middle- and upper-class culture and values. This means that the insights and values of any other group or subculture are often ignored. Ask the next Boomers you meet what their parents did for a living when they were growing up. If you find out these Boomers did not have professional, college-educated parents, ask if they have ever seen a movie or a television show that honestly depicted their youth or young-adult years.

It is critically important for all Boomers to reconcile important experiences from their past with their present because the third stage of our lives naturally brings with it major life-changing moments. We will all confront events that will never allow us to see ourselves in the same way ever again. Someone significant in our life will die. We'll find out a close friend has cancer. Our career path will take an unexpected turn because of a corporate merger. At these moments, we automatically begin to look much deeper within ourselves. And when we do, we can find real strength in the basic core values we grew up with.

"It is critically important for all Boomers to reconcile important experiences from their past with their present . . ."

It is also time to recognize what a tremendous accomplishment this group of Boomers, and their less-educated and less-cultured families, have made as group. America now boasts the largest and best-educated professional and paraprofessional group of men and women in human history ever to evolve from poor, working class, or small family-business roots.

Because of these origins and because of such shaping events as the Vietnam War, the civil rights movement, the sexual revolution, women's movement, and the longest and most continuous period of prosperity in American history, we also share to a greater or lesser degree, some key values. I've identified six:

Six Key Values of Baby Boomers

1. A sense of belonging

2. Giving something back

3. Taking risks

4. Entitlement

5. Expectations of the good life

6. Experimentation

If the six values described on the following pages are meaningful for you, you fit the description of most people in your generation. If you resonate with these values but are older than fifty-five or younger than thirty-seven, you can more easily relate to aging Boomers and feel free to ReFire right along side them.

1. A Sense of Belonging

Barbara Jensen, a psychologist, trainer, and university instructor, is one of very few people in the country writing and lecturing about the effects of working class roots in today's culture and on one's life journey. Barbara believes that one important key to understanding how the working-class culture is different from the middle- or upper-middle-class, lies in what she calls a "cultural sense of belonging." She believes *belonging* is best understood in contrast to *becoming,* (which Barbara connects more with a middle-class emphasis on individuality and achievement.) "Belonging," according to Barbara, "necessarily involves paying attention to and being part of the world around us." It is a powerful sense of identity that naturally and almost instinctively includes others around us, who wish that as we succeed, they will also. Belonging is not just thinking, abstracting, or discussing the world; it is jumping in with all of your gifts and limitations.

When Barbara and other working class Boomers were kids, there were many places where they felt like they belonged: in neighborhoods and neighbors' homes, bowling leagues, American Legion dances, skating parties, church and school youth groups, informal sports teams, public swimming pools, and so on.

There were, of course, young working class peers who did not feel as if they belonged. Some young Boomers who were homosexuals or others who were pushed by their parents to be more upwardly mobile vehemently say how they didn't feel like they "belonged" as young people. Their intensity about being outsiders underscores how important and deeply felt the sense of belonging was in the working class culture.

But the vast majority of working class Boomers knew that their acceptance was largely unconditional. It did not depend on what their parents did for a living or what kind of clothes they wore. There was always some comfortable place in the neighborhood or in the wider community where they were wanted and appreciated.

As adults, these working class Boomers struggle to fit in. They grumble about how pretentious an "in" restaurant is or how a shallow party conversation about something esoteric dragged on and on. Why is it that so many of us have reached high levels of professional and career success but still don't feel as if we belong? Many of us feel like the character Sonny in the novel *Losing Absalom* by Alexis D. Pate. He was an ambitious young black man on the path to executive status at the Data Central Corporation. But deep down Sonny carried a secret: he was afraid. Sonny really wondered if he truly belonged where he was, so far from where he came—the shadows of the inner city. And every time he thought about this, he became afraid that "one day someone would ask him to leave and go back home." It appears that all the corporate perks, athletic clubs, country clubs, and other formal and informal networks aren't meeting some of our deepest needs or fears. Will today's middle- or upper-middle-class Boomers from working class roots ever feel as comfortable as they did when they were kids?

ReFirement is about *belonging* as well as *becoming*. Every professional and paraprofessional from a working class background needs to begin sharing their "belonging" value with all of their coworkers, neighbors, members of their faith communities, and civic organiza-

> "ReFirement is about belonging as well as becoming."

tions. The contribution of the value of belonging will comfort many of those suffering from the pain of loneliness and isolation. More importantly, we will also be modeling how we want to be treated as we grow older.

2. Giving Something Back

As people who received much, and expect more, many Boomers are motivated to "give back" to the society. This concept of giving back is especially meaningful to Boomers of color who have come from poor neighborhoods.

Many of the young Boomers of color who grew up in poor families shared a strong value of belonging, because they lived in small towns or in confined areas of cities, where they had large extended families both by blood and kinship. Whenever they left their ghettos, almost all of them experienced racism and discrimination. They saw their own communities burn, police dogs tear into young children very much like themselves, innocent babies die in church bombings, and their principal leader, Dr. Martin Luther King, preach nonviolence only to have his life cut short by the violent act of an assassin.

Although the more dramatic moments of the civil rights struggle have been well documented in the popular media, its impact on young people of color who grew up during the late 1950s through the early 1970s has received little attention. Even though independent artists like Spike Lee (film producer/director) and Sandra Cisneros (Latina author) tell compelling real-life stories about their "hoods" and families to largely racial or ethnic audiences, most of white America knows very little about the rich and intricate web of networks and relationships in those economically distressed communities of the 1950s, '60s, and '70s and how they affected these young people growing up.

If you talk to many forty and fifty year olds of color about their childhood, they will say their formula for success was simple: Many people in their immediate and extended support networks sacrificed a great deal to help them make a better life for themselves. Many of them were only able to "make it" with the broad support of their wider community.

Elizabeth Higginbotham is an African American Boomer, a professor who grew up in such a community. She writes and lectures about upward mobility and African American women. In an article on "Moving Up with Kin and Community," she tells the stories of a number of professional African American women who grew up in the poor or lower working class. Some of these women were:

- A health investigator who says that no matter how much education or professional status she receives, she doesn't want to lose touch with where she's come from.

- A high-ranking city official who remembers that because she now has more opportunities, she has an obligation to give back more and set a positive example.

- The director of a social service agency who proudly says she owes a responsibility to her entire community.

Elizabeth's examples can be multiplied by the hundreds of thousands of minority men and women across the country. Many professionals of color are now working in the helping professions to empower present and future generations with the same opportunities they received while growing up.

Giving back is—and will be—an important value for all of us to consider as we age. Today only one in five seniors volunteers his or her time. With all of the challenges we face in the twenty-first century, Boomers across class and race need to join hands in developing healthy and safe communities.

"Boomers across class and race need to join hands in developing healthy and safe communities."

There are many good signs. Mentoring is now being supported in large corporations thanks largely to General Colin Powell, America's leading role model of "giving back." Elementary and high school students are being introduced to the concept of service through a variety of service learning programs. More communities of faith with aging populations are asking how they can become involved in community service.

Discovering how we can give back across race, culture, and ethnicity also provides a wonderful opportunity for an entire generation to begin a new dialogue on increasing community service in the new millennium.

3. Taking Risks

While taking risks is certainly something many of us did in our older teens or as younger adults, risk taking was a value many of us learned as young children if we grew up in a home where our parents owned a business such as a hardware store, restaurant, or a small family farm. Consciously or subconsciously, we were aware of how much our family risked each year, betting on their own entrepreneurial skills or on mother nature.

These families operated their small businesses for a wide variety of reasons. Most wanted to be their own bosses and stay independent. Many just liked to serve people in their neighborhood or community. And others owned a business or farm that was passed down from generation to generation.

Most of these families didn't really fit into the middle-class culture because they worked with their hands and with things—not with ideas and abstractions. At the same time, most of them did not enjoy great upward mobility or regularly increasing incomes. What did set them apart, however, is the fact that they owned and operated their own businesses.

Today there are countless stories of people who retire and discover the entrepreneurial bug. (It is difficult not to catch it in a society where commerce is king.) But one of the major problems these new/old entrepreneurs face is a lack of business experience or, more importantly, the personal will and commitment it takes to own and run their own company.

We know that many Boomers will not be financially able to retire at sixty-two or sixty-five or even seventy. For this reason many of us will want to take advantage of the exploding world of new home-based businesses. There is plenty of information on the Internet or in libraries about the techniques of starting your own business. But most successful small-business owners will tell you that how to incorporate or set up a bookkeeping system is not the most important information you will need to succeed.

It takes a certain kind of dedication and spirit to make it in any business. Fortunately many Boomers were first-hand witnesses to the secrets of making a living as your own boss. They need to share their first-hand stories about the entrepreneurial risk-taking spirit with other Boomers preparing for ReFirement.

I remember vividly my own family's experience with risks taken and abandoned. My father had an incredible work ethic. He started working in a scrap yard after the war. He swept floors and separated scrap that later went to the steel mills to be recycled. Like other G.I.s, he went to a business school at night to learn skills such as bookkeeping. For fifteen years my father worked six days a week, never taking a single day of vacation. Our first family vacation was a three-day trip to Lake Erie when I was sixteen years old!

During World War Two my father was an infantry cook in the army. After the war, as an Italian father, he loved to cook. Every Sunday (his only day off) he would make spaghetti, hot sausage, meatballs, and sauce for our family and friends. Sunday dinners were very special times. A dozen or more people sat around our dining room table enjoying great Italian food, drinking chianti, and talking nonstop about everything in the world. Everyone who came to eat said, "You should really sell that sauce of yours in those new supermarkets."

My dad desperately wanted to be his own boss. One day after Sunday mass, he and I went to large restaurant supply business. We bought two huge stainless steel caldrons to cook sauce. Next we went to a boat store where dad bought a set of oars and cut them down to use to stir the sauce in the caldrons. Then we proceeded to an Italian market where he bought large cans of peeled tomatoes, paste, fresh spices, ground meat, sausage, and pork. Finally, he bought a deep freezer and said, "Jimmy, we're going into the sauce business."

I didn't know quite what that meant, but I quickly realized it was a family affair. My two sisters, brother, and mother would gather in the kitchen after dinner, and watch my father make gallons of sauce. The smells were fantastic. We would then package the sauce in quart containers, stick labels on them with our new business name, *Vincento's Italian Sauces,* and deliver them to supermarkets where my father's samples had generated sales.

The business took off. We cooked five nights a week just to keep up with demand. Because our kitchen was not very big, my parents even thought about renting a larger kitchen. Then one day my father came home from work looking very worried. His boss had found out about his new venture and had made him an offer. He would give my father a promotion, a substantial raise, and buy him a new car. In exchange, my father would have to give up the sauce business.

What made matters worse was that we had just moved out of our working class neighborhood and built a new house in the suburbs. If my father chose the sauce business, it would mean giving up the house, changing schools, and cutting back our lifestyle. We took an informal vote in the family. My mother and two sisters voted for security and giving up the sauce business. My father and I voted to keep it. My father and I lost.

From that day (until fourteen years later when he finally opened up his own bar and restaurant), my father was an unhappy man. He put what he believed were the family's interests first and stopped taking risks.

The lesson here is that we need to follow our hearts when it comes to taking risks. Life is too short. We need to value risk taking and at the same time, honor the millions of Boomers who grew up in risk-taking environments.

". . . we need to follow our hearts when it comes to taking risks."

While the values of belonging, giving back, and risk taking are more strongly connected to poor, working class, and small business/farm families raising young Boomers in the 1950s, '60s and early '70s, these values are also found in some middle- and upper-middle-class homes raising children during the same time period. I have certainly met peers from the other twenty-five percent of our generation who share many of the same values with me. But the next three values better describe and reflect the experiences of our entire generation.

4. Entitlement

One description of Boomers is absolutely true: We are a generation of *entitlement*. We all grew up at a time of unparalleled prosperity and optimism.

> *"We are a generation of entitlement."*

During our lifetimes no major depression occurred. Our own family may not have been wealthy, but the overall postwar economy was booming during our formative years and continues to boom. Even if our family or community did not share directly in this prosperity, we, as the first television generation, daily viewed images of American affluence. We were weaned on advertising and learned quickly to shop— and consume—with gusto!

Besides growing up in a prosperous time, Boomers were privileged in additional ways that previous generations were not. Growing up in households that were largely child-focused, with mothers who had turned to the child-nurturing advice of Dr. Benjamin Spock, we assumed early on that we were special. Society focused on getting us a good

education. We were often the first people in all the generations of our families to finish high school, go to college or
trade school, or enter officer's candidate school in the military.

Many of us were taught to believe we were *entitled* to
meaningful jobs in order to enjoy the growing fruits of the
expanding economy and the new consumer products that
were emerging all around us. Previous generations were
largely limited by the needs for putting most of their efforts
toward economic and even physical survival. We were the
first generation with the luxury to focus on lifestyle choices.
It is no wonder we became a generation with large expectations.

5. Expectations of the Good Life

A spirit of entitlement leads to massive expectations. Not
only did we believe in unlimited access to education, good
jobs, and the consumer goods that flowed from these, but
our most important expectations have been about bringing
meaning to our lives and work. Our parents and grandparents, when they struggled to survive, did not have the luxury
of seeking meaning. Baby Boomers, however, have moved
beyond survival and limited possibilities into a new world of
abundance.

The focus on meaning has expressed itself through
Boomers in several important ways. Most obviously,
Boomers tend not to settle easily for mere income-
producing jobs. Instead, we expect meaningful work that
adds value to our inner lives. We sought jobs that were
"worth doing." We talked not just about "jobs" but about

"careers" and "career tracks," "continuing education," and "professional and paraprofessional development."

Most Boomers ignored the trades of our fathers to seek careers that we believed would bring us greater fulfillment and success. If early job choices did not meet our expectations, we simply traded them in for a better career fit.

Since adolescence, Boomers have also sought meaning through addressing the social issues of our time. We were late entrants in the civil rights movement but in the vanguard of the environmental, women's, and peace movements. If Boomers could not agree on the rightness of the Vietnam War, we could agree on its gross mishandling and government deception. We were disturbed that many of our peers who died or were wounded and sacrificed their innocence came home to an ungrateful and unsympathetic nation.

In all of these involvements, Boomers demonstrated a belief in our moral rectitude and superiority. The world was in bad shape and, as Boomers, we found meaning in trying to fix the world—and were confident we could do it.

But we also share a drive for discovering inner meaning beyond work and social issues. We have fueled the self-help, self-improvement, "higher consciousness" and twelve step movements. Throughout our lives, we have shared a strong emphasis on self, and we are rightly described as "self-absorbed." Boomers have earned the title of the "Me Generation," and now *self-fulfillment* and *self-actualization* are part of the mainstream cultural lexicon.

However, our expectations of continued abundance and of increased meaning have also contributed toward Boomers being the most stressed-out generation. Continued struggles with self-improvement and the inevitable mind-crunching reality of disappointments—when our romantic expectations turned to occasional dust—with divorce, job downsizing, drug use, and delinquency of our children. As millions of us move into midlife, the pressures of being the sandwich generation, (caught between an aging parent and younger children and grandchildren) and the seeming rigidity of political structures have taken their toll.

6. Experimentation

We have continued to be a generation of experimenters. As young people, some Boomers were visible protesters in the streets and on college campuses. Nearly all of us have been rule breakers in family life, workplace, and in the religious and political arenas. Over eighty percent of young Boomers experimented illegally with marijuana.

Largely freed from concerns about financial and physical survival and spurred on by our sheer numbers, we demand all kinds of changes in our society and local communities. We were weaned on change. We began to think of ourselves as change agents, bound to find new and better ways.

Our emphasis on individuality, our sense of specialness, and our expectations of success contributed toward a natural bent to experimentation. We felt safe in experimenting, less constrained than our parents about "fitting in." We would "do our own thing" like try drugs, grow long hair, and love rock and roll.

"Our emphasis on individuality, our sense of specialness, and our expectations of success contributed toward a natural bent to experimentation."

Our experimentation has also been fueled by a skepticism of authority and institutions born of youthful experiences with the Vietnam War, the violent deaths of the Kennedys, Martin Luther King Jr., and the students at Jackson State and Kent State—and later with Watergate.

We Boomers have repeatedly experimented in our quest for inner meaning, which has led many away from traditional churches and synagogues to experiences with Eastern traditions, New Age movements, and evangelistic religion. Perhaps Boomers are best described as a generation of individuals who "pick and choose" their spiritual practices. Someone wrote that Boomers "built churches in the privacy of their own heads."

In addition to these six core values, there are many other important values we need to draw from our childhoods as we grow older. As young people most of us learned to respect our elders, not to shame others, to believe in spiritual as well as material needs, and to distrust institutional hierarchies because we saw how our parents were treated by large organizations and institutions. Many of our parents taught us to be "down to earth," trust our common sense, have compassion for the underdog, and to expect caring and cooperation in our communities as a normal part of everyday life.

The question of who the Boomers are will not be answered in our lifetimes. Historians and sociologists will continue to debate the impact and legacy of our generation on American history for decades to come. The one issue that nobody can debate is that all of us are aging, and the fact alone will dominate the immediate political, social, and cultural arenas of American life.

What Your Parents Really Meant

A friend of mine said she had a problem with something her mother always told her as a young girl. Her
mother said, "Now Judy, you just be a nice girl." As
she grew up and became a feminist and union leader,
she resented the "nice girl" advice because she felt it
contradicted being a strong and independent
thinking woman. Now at midlife she realizes that
being a nice girl could also have meant being more
compassionate or empathetic. Make a list of things
your parents told you when you were growing up.
Can any of them can be be redefined to help you
better understand yourself at this stage in your life?

A note of caution: We should not romanticize any particular
set of values. Many Boomers who grew up as poor, working
class, or as members of a family-owned business, also
understood the limitations and the pains they suffered
because of cultural or economic deprivation. Understanding
where we come from is far different than taking a trip down
nostalgia lane. Boomers can now get on with the business of
reconnecting with their past and personal history in new
and positive ways. The growing wisdom and experience of
age will naturally help us pick and choose the best from our
backgrounds and hopefully leave our major mistakes
behind.

We cannot escape our family roots. We can finally begin to tell our own stories without shame or guilt. Everyone can be proud of the assets we collectively bring to the aging society.

The important Baby Boomer values identified in this chapter do not match with current attitudes about aging and retirement. Something has to give. And the first major test of a successful ReFirement will be to honestly and maturely accept our own aging.

Activities to ReFire your life

Connecting with Your Values

Review the list of ReFirement principles and values below. Beside each one, complete this sentence: "When I hear the word(s) _____ [ReFirement word], I think of _____ [your thought], I feel _____ [your emotion], and I want to _____ [your personal action]."

When you have finished, go back and list an example of when you experienced each of these ReFirement principles. Then, look at what you have written and see what pattern you can discern in your responses. This can also be fun to do with others.

Entitlement
Expectations
Belonging
Giving back
Experimenting
Risk taking

Clarify Your Values

This involves a simple test. For example, let's say you took the value of "Giving Something Back." How did you choose that value? Is it something you do on a regular basis? Do you do it because you really want to? Do you plan on doing it for a long time? Are you willing to publicly promote this activity? If you can answer a passionate yes to each one of these questions, that value is true to you.

The Next 30 Years

As you think about the next thirty years of your life, what values do you think will be most important to you?

Activities to **ReFire** your life

Make an Accumulation Inventory

Many businesses are required to do an inventory of their entire stock annually. Most of us never do an inventory of our own possessions even *once* in a lifetime. Midlife can be a good time to do our own inventory. This will help you explore a number of the values from this chapter.

Get yourself a little notebook or use a handheld computer or tape recorder. Go from room to room in your home and make note of your possessions. Check those objects you still use. Then prioritize items to indicate their current value. A simple A, B, C system will work—or devise your own coding system. Don't forget to inventory items in your office, garage, and car.

When you are finished, choose at least a dozen low-priority possessions to let go—then give them away! Then, select another dozen and keep track of whether you use them during the next six months. If you don't use them, consider giving them away too.

Next, choose a dozen of your most valued treasures among all the things you own. Why are they important to you? If you want to take this exercise further, tell someone about the history you share with each possession. Perhaps make this a "show and tell" and share your treasures and stories. Even better, choose to share them with a person from another generation. If any of these things were gifts, again thank the person who gave them to you. Finally, decide whom you would like to have each of these items when you die.

Chapter 2

Turning Aging Upside Down

True to my Baby Boomer roots, I thought I was more or less immortal—until I hit my mid-forties and began to see signs of my mortality. After playing eighteen holes on a difficult golf course, my body suddenly needed two pain relievers and one complete day to recuperate.

When I turned forty-five, I also began to struggle with birthdays. You see, the year before my father died suddenly. I was not prepared for the impact his death would have on my life. Two years after his death I was making a business presentation when something that was said made me break down in tears and leave the room. Now I know why. A friend helped me make sense of my birthday anxiety by saying, "When a parent dies, the magma shifts." When the magma shifts under the earth you don't see or hear it but the earthquakes and volcanoes it can cause are quick reminders of its immense power.

On each birthday since my father's death, I had consciously or unconsciously revisited some of my life goals that still remained unfulfilled. Each birthday made me confront looming and perplexing questions surrounding my own aging.

I don't think I'm alone. Most Baby Boomers will soon experience the death of a parent or some other major life crisis. When their "magma shifts," the questions will start:

- What does it really mean to get older?
- What have I accomplished?
- Am I making a difference?
- Is the daily stress I put myself through really worth it?
- How will I spend the rest of my life?
- Will I be able to live a long and happy life financially, physically, mentally, and spiritually?

Prompted by these questions, I listed all of the things that I feared most about getting older. The list included:

- physical limitations and illnesses
- losing the ability to live independently
- losing the ability to drive
- lack of savings
- living longer than my wife
- not living longer than my wife
- losing respect
- dementia
- loneliness
- not having my own biological children
- not being as significant as I am now
- losing my youthful appearance
- mistreatment at the hands of others
- death

Of all the things I feared about getting older, *becoming insignificant and losing respect* outweighed even my fears of illness and death. I wondered if my business and life's work would suffer as I hit sixty-five and seventy because clients might view me as out of touch with current trends. I considered whether young people would value my accumulated wisdom or simply disregard me as an old man who could offer neither understanding nor creativity about issues of importance to them.

"Of all the things I feared about getting older, becoming in-significant and losing respect outweighed even my fears of illness and death."

Sometimes my approach to difficult or unfinished business is very Boomer-like. As a true Boomer, I make a list of what needs to be done and feel I have a handle on the problem. Then the list usually gets buried under my other lists.

My "fear of aging" list was different. It wasn't about just naming something and trying to figure out what to do to take off the pressure. It went deeper—much, much deeper. At least I was finally getting honest about my own aging, and I had named some of my real fears. I realized that accepting my own aging was hard work and would take a lifetime—but at least I had begun.

If we can break through our denial of aging and obsession with remaining young, we may find that some of our common values and history as a generation can be reframed to both our own advantage and that of the larger culture in which we will live out our lives in the coming years.

Your Fear of Aging List

Take some time alone in a place where you can relax. Give yourself five minutes to write down your responses to the following question: "What am I afraid of as I get older?"

After five minutes, review your list. Add to it as you wish. Then set it aside and take a break.

When you return, review the list again and make changes.

Finally, using the following code, indicate the degree of your fear:

A= Absolute panic; B= Pretty scary;
C= Frightens me some, but I already
see strategies on how to deal with
this one.

In a notebook, write a fear at the top of each page and gradually begin to note strategies you might employ to cope with each of your fears. If you are comfortable doing so, invite your significant other, a sibling, or friends to develop lists too. Share them with each other and, together, brainstorm coping devices.

During the next six months, revisit your fear list at least every other week. Add or subtract from it or change the coding based on your current feelings.

This exercise can help you to confront the reality of your aging process and help you to begin to find strategies for ReFiring. You will likely discover that you gradually find each of the fears on your list a little less frightening.

Some facts you may not want to know

The total market for cosmetic-enhancement products and procedures in the United States is currently nearly $100 billion a year and is anticipated to become a trillion-dollar business because of the aging Baby Boomer market. These enhancements included antibaldness "solutions," aesthetic surgery, nonsurgical lifts, and liposuctions. This industry is directed to both women and men. In fact, the most popular male vanity procedure today for men over sixty is a "butt lift"!

There is also a growing practice called "anti-aging medicine." This field includes aesthetic surgery, restorative dentistry, and cosmetic dermatology. The following is advertising copy from a very expensive and glossy marketing magazine produced in Canada. It is distributed internationally to medical and dental offices:

> The first faint lines appear at the corner of your eyes or above your upper lip. It must be a mistake. This can't be happening to you. But slowly . . . your skin begins to show signs of age—wrinkles, discoloration, and loose jowly skin. The good news is you're not alone. As millions of Baby Boomers see wrinkles instead of acne, the cosmetic and drug companies are working furiously to develop various anti-aging products from dietary supplements to face creams and chemical peels, that may help slow or even prevent the effects of aging.

It is admirable for Boomers to want to take care of their bodies, stay fit, rejuvenate their character, and reconnect with their spirituality. But people in the cosmetic and drug business are counting on Boomers being hell bent on keeping their youthful appearance as long as possible. We are being sold the old "fountain of youth" in an enticing and sophisticated new package. And we are paying a tremendous economic and social cost for denying our own aging.

The $100 billion a year to make ourselves look better represents a little more than $4000 for every man, woman, and child in the U.S. This $100 billion is almost equivalent to the entire amount of money given through individual and corporate philanthropy every year. Moreover, it is nearly the entire gross national product of Greece, Hungary, Austria, and Denmark combined! If you decided to count from one to 100 billion starting today, it would take you and many other generations about 95,000 years.

In addition to the question of how we use disposable income, there is an even more serious side of age denial. Whether we like it or not, the young naturally and instinctively look to the old for wisdom, advice, and mentorship. Imagine how confusing it is for young people to see people of the age of fifty or sixty trying to look and act as if they are in their twenties or thirties.

As a human species we still need to maintain the natural balance and cycle of life. Maggie Kuhn, a personal friend and founder of the Gray Panthers, said, "Everything that lives, all of the plants and animals—including the human animal—are born of seed, flourish and bear fruit or progeny, wither, and die." It's important that we learn to accept our own mortality and be more grateful for the time we have to enjoy life's many wonders.

Boomers are a difficult group to satisfy. We want it all. We want to retain our youth while being respected for our years of experience. But in reality, there are payoffs for gracefully accepting our own aging. According to author and social

futurist, Betty Friedan, a truly maturing Boomer cohort—
one that chooses to ignore all of the anti-aging advertising
and "fountain of youth" promises—accepting our own aging
will cause a social revolution in the United States that will
rival the accomplishments of all of the major social movements in U.S. history.

Activities to ReFire your life

Picture Your Aging

Gather your family picture albums. Organize the
photos so they show you or your entire family at
different ages. Arrange the pictures so that they
demonstrate your aging process and that of your
family and friends. Then look at the pictures carefully.
Recall the situations in which they were taken and the
memories they trigger. As you review the photos, pay
attention to your emotions.

Do this as a family activity or share your pictures
with a friend or colleague. Tell stories about the
pictures. Encourage each person to share what they
remember about the situation or the time in which a
picture was taken. When you have finished, you may
want to summarize your thoughts and feelings in your
ReFirement journal or on tape. Share them with
another person if that feels right.

Do you see the Boomer values of entitlement,
expectation, experimentation, belonging, giving back,
or risk taking in your pictures?

Living Intergenerationally, the Best Way to Age

The best strategy, and certainly the most economical one, for keeping a youthful spirit is to be intentional about connecting with other generations younger and older than yourself. I have the great opportunity in my work to travel around the country and bring all our five living generations together to dialogue and solve problems or create new opportunities. I do this in communities, corporations, and in faith communities. It never ceases to amaze me, after eight years and more than 110 intergenerational dialogue events, how much people of all ages are hungering for an authentic connection with each other and how desperately our society needs this connection.

Here are some other disturbing facts

- Several summers ago in Chicago, more than 350 elder citizens (mostly minorities on fixed incomes) died from heat suffocation because they were too afraid to leave their own apartments and ask for help.
- Suicide rates in the U.S. among teen and the elderly are the highest in the industrialized world.
- The fastest growing form of segregation in this country is age segregation (particularly in senior-only retirement communities).
- All over the country, school bond referenda are being defeated because senior citizens either question the ability of the schools to educate or believe young people living in their communities are no longer an important part of their lives.

Many older Americans, across class, race, and gender, talk about their fears of young people. They believe they no longer have much of a personal connection to younger generations, except in places where the young work or through what the elders see on television. A social service agency in a predominately African American neighborhood in Peoria, Illinois, thought it would be a good idea to get young teens to help older people with yard cleanup, house painting, and other maintenance chores. The program never got off the ground because many of the African American elders were afraid of the young teenage strangers.

Many teenagers are isolated from older adults. The "teen culture" so prominently displayed on MTV and the horde of new teen dramas and sitcoms on TV make it appear that teenagers and young people in general live in a generational vacuum. They are always with each other, receive advice only from peers, and live their lives apart from any positive or significant adult role models. The *only* commonality found among the young people involved in the recent spate of school shootings is that not one of them had a significant adult in their lives with whom they could have shared the obvious turmoil going on inside them.

Whether taken singly or collectively, these facts are not healthy signs for an aging population that is about to increase by seventy-six million Baby Boomers.

When we decide to become more intentionally intergenerational about our lives, we automatically become both historians and futurists. We look to history and to those older than we in order to secure a context for understanding our own lives and the society in which we live. We look to younger people—and even to generations yet unborn—to catch a glimpse of our future.

I attended the National Foster Grandparents Conference in Orlando, Florida. A friend of mine asked me to come to the awards celebration and meet some of the best examples of people who choose to live in an intentional intergenerational way.

"When we decide to become more intentionally intergenerational about our lives, we automatically become both historians and futurists."

Harold was a retiree who first volunteered as a foster grandparent to read to elementary and kindergarten children in public schools. One day he came home and told his wife he was changing his job to work with teenagers who were ordered by a court to an alternative education program. Worried about his safety, all of his friends and even his family discouraged him. They felt he would be "completely out of his element." But Harold said this would be a great challenge for a seventy-three year old. There were young people who didn't have anyone in their lives, and he was just going to be there for them.

Robert, Harold's foster grandson, was sixteen and had been expelled from high school. By all accounts, he was on a very bad path to adulthood. Harold spent the next two years just being there for Robert when he needed him. They became good friends and shared many personal moments. Robert's life began to turn around. He renewed his interest in school and, with Harry's help, got out of the alternative program, graduated from his former high school, and found a good job.

A week after Harold found out he and Robert were going to be nationally honored at the Foster Grandparent's conference, Harold had a massive heart attack and died. Harold's wife and and Robert accepted the award. There was not a dry eye in the audience. They both talked about how young Harold seemed and how much energy he always had for his volunteering. Even when he was not physically feeling well, somehow he would recover when it was time to be with Robert. During his time as a foster grandparent, Harold kept a drawer full of notes he wrote. On one of them he wrote, "We should not be judged in the end on what we have, but rather on what we do with what we have."

Harold's gifts and courage show what can happen when age differences are accepted and valued in a relationship. Harold didn't need any anti-aging creams or lotions to stay young and relevant.

My own attitudes on aging have changed dramatically over the past eight years because of my intergenerational work. During one of my intergenerational dialogues, a twelve year old came up to me and said, "Thank you, Dr. Gambone. Nobody has ever asked me an important question before." An elder woman in another dialogue told me she was feeling isolated and lonely. She hadn't talked directly to a teenager for over ten years! And a Boomer related how wonderful it was to be put in a situation in which he had to listen to four other generations communicate their feelings and concerns.

I have learned that every generation has unique gifts, perspectives, talents, and limitations. When they are honest with each other and respect each other's differences, they can work together to try and find some solutions. As more generations are involved in dialogue, the greater chance exists that an impressive array of intergenerational solutions will be developed and acted upon.

If ReFiring Boomers want to stay young, all they have to do is make a commitment to practice basic respect, caring, and cooperation with all generations. Such efforts automatically promote the values of belonging, risktaking, and giving back. Yet, we can experiment even further and develop new ways of reaching out and understanding other generational perspectives and concerns. Boomers in ReFirement can accept their own aging, reverse the trend toward generational segregation, and be in the vanguard of promoting understanding and collaboration among all the living generations.

As you will see in the next chapter, accepting our own aging will be much easier when we decide as a generation to end the current retirement system and retire retirement!

Activities to ReFire your life

How Many Ages Do You Relate To?

Outside of your immediate family, do you have a significant relationship with someone from a different generation? If you do, how do you talk about that relationship with others? If you don't, try to develop a friendship with someone older or younger than yourself.

Chapter 3

Let's Retire Retirement!

In 1996, when the leading edge Baby Boomers turned fifty, a media frenzy surrounded this momentous event. Being one of these leading edge Boomers, I came to believe that my fiftieth birthday was part of a dark conspiracy between greeting card companies, black balloon manufacturers, financial advisors, and gerontologists.

Even so, I tried to approach fifty as an optimistic and positive person in relatively good physical and mental health. The small business my wife and I own was paying the bills, even though as entrepreneurs, we are always exchanging security for freedom. Every month we wonder whether our income will match our expenses.

In employment, in my entire lifestyle, I am different from my parents and most of their generation. So when I looked around for inspiration on how to spend the last third of my life, I was disappointed. Traditional retirement planning messages really turned me off. A growing multibillion dollar financial planning industry was telling Boomers the same things they told our parents: invest wisely now for free time later.

But what if we want that free time now? Why should we wait to do what we really want to be doing? What price are we paying for enduring the stress of our current lifestyle on the bet that life in retirement will be more meaningful and happy? And what about the millions of Baby Boomers who don't want to quit working or won't be able to quit?

As a generation, we need to raise and answer important questions beyond the scope of current financial planning retirement models. A generation in the forefront of political, cultural, and economic change for the past fifty years should be creating new rules and visions for their journey into elderhood.

I believe that traditional retirement carries the wrong messages for all Americans. People between fifty and ninety, regardless of their physical condition, should not be forced to quit working and disengage from society or the culture. This is precisely the time to become more engaged. Seventy-six million Boomers have far too much to offer than spending the next thirty or forty years golfing in Sun City or Leisure World.

I believe that retirement is an outdated concept that will not meet the needs nor fit the values, experiences, and aspirations of this generation. We should not be wasting time trying to "redefine retirement" or "Boomerize it." **It is time we ended the retirement system for ourselves and for future generations.**

> *"I believe that retirement is an outdated concept that will not meet the needs nor fit the values, experiences, and aspirations of this generation."*

The dictionary says that a "retiree" is one who has "withdrawn from active duty or from one's career." Media-portrayed images of retirement often bounce between two extremes: pictures of hunched over elderly men and women sitting in run-down, cold apartment buildings or well-coifed gray-haired couples in brightly-colored sports clothes swinging golf clubs on a lovely green near their upscale home in some perfect retirement community. These images—representing our fears of scarcity and our pictures of the so-called "good life"—often war at the edge of our consciousness today.

I want to suggest some alternative images, but first let's briefly look at the current system.

Activities to ReFire your life

You Choose: Retirement or ReFirement?

Do you like the word "retirement"? Do you want to be referred to as a "retiree" or a "senior retiree"? Why or why not?

Today's Retirement System

Today's retirement system is relatively new.
It is only about five decades old. (Television has been around longer.) During the first quarter of the twentieth century, some thinkers and researchers believed that the mental and physical capacity of most people so seriously declined by their early sixties, they were no longer fit for the work force. In the United States, various state commissions, state and federal workers' pension programs, and railroad retirement programs chose the age of sixty-five as the beginning of eligibility for benefits.

In 1935, the earliest form of Social Security old age insurance covered only about forty-three percent of the population and excluded government, agricultural, and domestic workers, as well as the self-employed. The benefits provided were much more limited than today, but over the years eligibility was liberalized and benefits were expanded. Sharp increases occurred between 1950 and 1960, and in the mid-1960s, when Medicare and Medicaid were enacted.

Changes in the shape and extent of the largest entitlement programs have continued to this day. There never has been a grand retirement scheme. America's retirement practices simply evolved in fits and spurts. During the last decade, the debate has grown louder about these programs and recently has focused largely on the projected crises in funding them.

Government-managed retirement programs originally arose to create a safety net for an industrial work force, assuming that people's productive usefulness was concluded by their early to mid-sixties. One retirement expert said, "Retirement was created because organizations needed a mechanism to control entry and departure into the working world. . . . Retirement quickly became society's formal mechanism to endorse, regulate, and sanction the removal of the elderly from the paid labor force."

Moreover, the current retirement system emerged at a time when there were far more young workers than retirees and when human life expectancy was considerably shorter than it is now. Neither politicians nor lobbying groups considered that the time would come when there would be fewer young workers than the number of retirees. Nor did they predict that growing life expectancies would greatly extend the lengths of people's retirement.

In short, the basic outline of today's retirement system grew incrementally and haphazardly over a half century or more, its roots in a very different demographic and cultural reality than we encounter today.

Retirement doesn't fit the needs of today's women.

The retirement system emerged to serve the needs of men, who composed the bulk of the labor market at the time when the seeds of today's retirement practices were planted. For example, in 1940, women made up less than one-fourth of the total labor force. It was assumed that retirement practices served women as well as men, because women were married to men who retired. Even those women who were employed usually worked at part-time or lower-paying jobs that merely supplemented their husbands' salaries.

The entire system was built on the assumption of a married couple living out the last few years of their lives with a safety net that allowed them to avoid poverty. Over the last fifty years, however, marriage, family, and employment patterns have shifted radically. Most Boomer women work outside the home. The four-person nuclear family no longer predominates in our culture—and hasn't for many years. More than fifty percent of marriages end in divorce. Millions of women are single heads of households, raising children, and others are single by choice over a lifetime or due to delayed marriages or divorce.

Moreover, nearly half of these women hold low-paying jobs on which their Social Security and pension benefits are based. It is estimated, for example, that female retirees receive only half the average pension benefits of men. Also, currently women outlive their male partners or counterparts by an average of nearly fifteen years and thereby have a much extended retirement period.

The retirement system that emerged five decades ago did not anticipate the large numbers of women in the labor force, the number of female heads of household, nor the longevity of women. It also did not take into adequate account the influence of ongoing gender discrimination, glass ceilings, or the movement of women in and out of the work force to care for children and aging parents. (Chapter 7, "Healing Divisions In Our Society," explores some of the great challenges Boomer women will face if the current retirement culture continues.)

Retirement isn't working for current retirees.

On the first day of the new millennium one of the lead stories on national television news was that people over age sixty-five have the highest suicide rate in the nation and more than two million of them suffer from severe depression. Some researchers are also uncovering high rates of drug and alcohol use in age-segregated communities. Such alarming statistics do not speak well for the effectiveness of today's typical retirement lifestyles.

Most writers on aging and current retirement practices express major concerns. Some argue against forced retirement, others against raising the retirement age, and still others warn of the inequities of a system that provides monthly financial transfers from younger, working-poor families to elderly millionaires and other elders who don't need financial help.

One retiree summed it up better than any Boomer ever could. He said retirement is based on a faulty concept of human nature and the relationship of men and women to the larger society. Retirement is, he said, "inhumane, erroneous, retrogressive, bad for the health and well-being of retirees, ruinously expensive for the nation, and probably immoral."

The office retirement party and its aftermath come as a traumatic shock for millions of men and women. We all know people in our families or friendship groups who become restless and bored soon after the initial vacation or rounds of golf are complete, men who get underfoot at home creating a high level of stress for their wives and families, or those who die shortly after retiring. "And he was so looking forward to his retirement," we mutter in disbelief.

The stress of such a dramatic change in lifestyle and shift in one's self-worth and identity is complicated by the fact that society expects recent retirees to be positively giddy in relief at leaving their jobs, exulting in a new life of freedom and leisure. Their fellow working Americans do not want to hear them complain about their new lives. Even those retirees who seem to have done the best preparation for retirement—carefully saving and achieving a bulging financial portfolio, buying a luxury home in a touted retirement community, and traveling widely—often become unhappy or restless within just a few years.

Retirement will not be hard to eliminate.

As our generation moves toward our sixties, there is a growing restlessness in the land about our current understanding and system of retirement. The congress and the executive branch, both dominated by aging Boomers, recently dismantled an important economic underpinning of retirement when they eliminated the amount of money someone can earn and still receive their full Social Security benefits. This kind of questioning and growing attention to disturbing statistics and trends foreshadows even greater changes to come. Approaching the retirement stage are seventy-six million men and women who have changed every other aspect of American life and culture. Surely the current retirement mindset and practices, as America has known them in recent decades, are about to be revised!

Activities to ReFire your life

Are Current Retirees Happy?

Think about four people you know who are retired. Are they happy? Why or why not?

Boomers Retire? No Way!

There is no reason to believe that Boomers can't or won't eliminate retirement in favor of a better way to spend their older years. An important survey conducted by Roper Research in 1998 for the American Association of Retired Persons (AARP) gives us clues about why retirement is particularly ill-suited for Boomers.

In the most extensive poll done to date of Baby Boomers' attitudes toward retirement, the AARP reported that eighty percent of Boomers expect to continue working during their retirement years. These Boomers say they wish to continue in the work force for the satisfaction work provides, or for the financial rewards they receive—or for both reasons.

The same 1998 AARP survey also
showed that nearly twenty-five
million Boomers do not expect to be
able to stop working because it will
be financially impossible for them to
do so. These men and women are
very concerned about income and
health-care coverage in their retirement years.

". . . nearly twenty-five million Boomers do not expect to be able to stop working because it will be financially impossible for them to do so."

Boomers across the nation are
also fueling today's rapid growth in home-based businesses.
Now that informational technology allows us to do worldwide marketing without leaving our homes, new home-
based businesses are a natural for Boomers in midlife and
older years.

Many of us are already seeking second careers and new
styles of work life. These activities are viewed as an adventure for those of us who have always been ready to experiment with new endeavors. These business movements and
workstyle experimentations suggest that retirement at an
arbitrary age is already an obsolete concept.

Respondents to the AARP poll overwhelming concluded
that they do not view retirement as the end of their productive years. As a generation, we will never tolerate being
considered less productive and relevant just because we
have reached a certain age. Such an outdated scenario
would require us to disengage at a time in our lives when we
realize we have the most expertise and wisdom to offer
society. Remember, we have always had high expectations
about our lives and the importance of our role in the culture
as change agents. Our older years will provide new freedoms
and arenas in which we will experiment, achieve, contribute,
and belong.

Although some of us will want to give back to society through volunteer efforts as well as through forms of paid employment, we are unlikely to settle for marginal volunteer opportunities and influence. With our education, skills, and sense of entitlement, many of us will expect to be in the center of the volunteer action in influential positions that we may have helped to create.

"With our educa-tion, skills, and sense of entitle-ment many of us will expect to be in the center of the volunteer action in influen-tial positions that we may have helped to create."

The changing forms of volun-teerism in recent years have, in fact, been largely shaped by the expecta-tions of Boomers. As we age, we will continue to mold community service. Most of us will not see our volunteer efforts as a substitute for the recognition and meaning that paid employment affords us. Instead, we will view volunteerism as an arena to bring added value to our society and to our own lives.

Until now, special age-segregation covenants, (allowed by an amendment to the Fair Housing Act) have enabled places like the Sun Cities of America to engage in actual age segre-gation without public outcries. Boomers are clear that we do not want our retirement to bring dependence on others or isolation from the rest of society. We are unlikely to tolerate living in age-segregated communities with older peers, away from the action of the larger society. For us, segregation based on age would spell dismissal and irrelevance, and that will never fit our self-image. We know we can have little influence on society as a whole if we are labeled as "active adults" living in "adult-oriented retirement communities." In order to continue to be important players in society, we will need to live and belong in intergenerational communities.

Finally, we are among those most aware that our current Social Security and Medicare systems are in severe financial danger. Emerging demographics and congressional reports support this concern. Social Security started at a time when younger workers far outnumbered people who were retiring. Without a major change in the system, when seventy-six million Boomers reach the current retirement age, fewer younger workers will be left with the burden of supporting people in long retirements as life expectancy rates are extended. Boomers are just beginning as a generation to find the political will to deal honestly with this issue. We cannot retire from our political activism.

While most people agree a strong safety net must be provided for older people who would otherwise be poor, frail, or lacking in health care services, younger workers are currently spending large portions of their incomes to provide benefits to many older people who are already relatively wealthy. This state of affairs is gradually setting up intergenerational conflict on an escalating scale.

Another kind of intergenerational tension arises when retirees feel they have already paid for their own children's education and community facilities and now refuse to approve bond issues for school buildings and educational opportunities for today's youth. Some seniors, for a wide variety of reasons, no longer see youth as part of their responsibility.

Yet the very youth whose education such older people refuse to support will one day soon be expected to supply the Social Security funds for the current retirement system. At a time when the collaboration of all people in our society is needed to solve challenging social issues and respond to exciting new possibilities, generations are becoming increasingly suspicious of one another.

I challenge my generation as part of their ReFirement to inaugurate a new intergenerational dialogue to decide on how we can retire retirement. This dialogue should be based on using our common sense and asking questions like:

> *"I challenge my generation as part of their ReFirement to inaugurate a new intergenerational dialogue to decide on how we can retire retirement."*

- What kind of resources will we need over the next thirty years to meet the needs of our aging population?

- What would it take to guarantee that everyone is able to live out their lives with dignity and respect?

- What is really fair and equitable to all generations?

The national intergenerational dialogue should begin immediately. By starting from the perspective of asking everyone to first help define how we all want to age and then to figure out how we can get there, new ways of thinking about aging will certainly emerge. This new ReFirement vision can bring generations together and encourage the release of our collective creativity, wisdom, and energy. What better way to bring new hope to our world in this new century?

Activities
to ReFire
your life

Bottom Lines in Old Age

If you had to pick three "bottom lines" (the minimum guarantees you want as an older American) for your elder years, what would they be?

Gender Differences and Retirement

Make a list of the differences between how men and women approach traditional retirement. Talk about these differences with someone of a different gender.

Chart Your Life's Dreams

Imagine that you'll live to be 100. It's possible! Trace the shape of your life so far and dream about how you'd like the rest of your life to look. What do you see yourself doing? Where will you live? Who will you be with?

1–10	51–60
11–20	61–70
21–30	71–80
31–40	81–90
41–50	91–100

Chapter 4

Getting Your Groove Back

The dictionary defines groovy as "very pleasing, attractive, a generalized term of approval, working effortlessly." Many of us connect the word with the song and what it was like to "feel groovy on a Tuesday afternoon."

I'd be willing to bet, however, there are few Boomers today who are feeling groovy on a Tuesday or on any other day of the week for that matter. Many of us seem to have lost that affirming, pleasing, and effortless feeling about life we had when we were younger. The loss is about something deeper than simply leaving behind the youthful 1960s and 1970s for the more responsible '80s, '90s, and the new century. As a group we appear somber ("heavy" in our own vernacular), with a more cynical approach to the world around us. Daniel Okrent, writing in *Time* magazine, painted an extremely bleak picture of our present condition.

If you're like the overwhelming majority of Boomers, your career has hit a brick wall, you haven't saved enough, . . . your health is deteriorating. . . . Need more? There are no movies made for people your age, the music on the radio is dreadful, television programmers behave as if you don't exist. . . . And stock market analysts are growing bullish on companies that build nursing homes or manufacture laxatives. Coming soon: the Metamucil boom. Here's looking at you kid.

How can we change the perception of what Okrent and others are saying about us? First, we have to admit that some of the criticism is "right on."

It is true that while our activity level has significantly increased over the past twenty to twenty-five years, our enjoyment and happiness quotient seems to be plummeting. You've heard the saying, "We seem to be doing more but enjoying it less." How many people do you know who really enjoy what they are doing? How often do you hear someone say how stuck they are and regretful because of some past life decision? And how many of your friends talk with excitement and confidence about the future? Getting our groove back means creating an environment in which people can experience happiness on a regular basis in their daily lives, keep regrets about their past from inhibiting their ability to change, and look to the future with excitement and passion.

> "Getting our groove back means creating an environment in which people can experience happiness on a regular basis in their daily lives, keep regrets about their past from inhibiting their ability to change, and look to the future with excitement and passion."

In his bestselling book called *Flow: The Psychology of Optimal Experience,* Mihaly Csikszentmihaly (his friends call him Mike) says the optimal moments of life experience usually occur when our body or mind are stretched to their limit in some activity we love to do. We literally forget ourselves and, in a state of almost unconscious activity, accomplish difficult and even worthwhile objectives.

One of my heroes, psychiatrist and death-camp survivor Dr. Viktor Frankl, put it another way, "Don't aim at success—

the more you aim at it and make it a target, the more you are going to miss it. For success, like happiness, cannot be pursued: it must ensue . . . as the unintended side effect of one's personal dedication to a cause greater than oneself."

In 1999 the Minneapolis *Tribune* ran an editorial, "The Golf Lesson." As a golfer, and someone trying to get his own groove back, I resonate to these words:

> A person is intrigued by the difficulty of the golf swing and his inability to fashion consistency. The longer he fidgets with a dozen small adjustments, the longer the odds that any good will come of it. The more he or she empties out all they have heard and read, the more likely some magic will occur. A joyful person does something without worry, without expectation, without striving.

I am a fifteen-handicap golfer, which means I am rarely consistent and seem to be always be making adjustments to my game. Not long ago I experienced the magic of Mihaly's optimal-experience flow. Over three difficult holes, I was able to shoot par. For those of you unfamiliar with golf, if I shot par on a regular basis, I wouldn't be writing books but playing on the professional senior tour. For a little over an hour—but for what seemed an eternity—I found myself in a very special zone. There was very little thinking involved— just a pure feeling of enjoyment on making good contact with the ball and overcoming any difficulty a hole presented. I felt no pressure, even though I had never made three pars in a row in fifteen years of playing golf. When my string finally ended on the fourth hole after I missed another par putt by inches, I took a deep breath, smiled, and felt very good about what I had accomplished. I knew somewhere deep within me were the skills and swing of a golfer who could shoot par over an extended number of holes. For a brief shining moment on that golf course, I discovered abilities I never knew I possessed. I was really in a "great groove," and I believed it could happen again.

Getting your groove back deals with being able to lighten up a little, find things you really like to do that also challenge you, help lose yourself and the frustrations of everyday life whenever you can, and experience the pure joy of what it feels like when you annihilate time.

Many of us have barely uncovered the many gifts we possess and the good things about ourselves that will help us prepare for our ReFirement. With a little self-searching, all of us will find hidden talents, aspirations, potentials, and possibilities that will get us excited about life and make us happier in the process. William Miller called this personal introspection "rediscovering your Golden Shadow," the private side of you that is "a source of power and possibility that we can bring into consciousness and use creatively and constructively for a fuller and more enriching experience of life." Some of us will discover our Golden Shadow through sports, the arts, dance, acting, gardening, creative writing, mentoring, or any other activity that really interests us.

ReFirement and our Boomer values tell you now is the time to experiment, take risks, and enjoy your gifts, whatever they are, every day of your life.

> *"ReFirement and our Boomer values tell you now is the time to experiment, take risks, and enjoy your gifts . . ."*

Three specific tools everyone can use to help get their groove back are: music, humor, and developing a greater sense of adventure about your life.

Music

Oliver Sacks, who some people call a "romantic neurologist," wrote the book *Awakenings* (you may know it through the Robin Williams movie by the same title). In another best seller, *The Man Who Mistook His Wife for a Hat and Other Clinical Tales,* Sacks tells the story of Martin, a patient whom he met in an "old folks home" in New York City. Martin was sixty-one and suffering from Parkinson's disease. As a child, he had been diagnosed as retarded and was cruelly treated all of his life. Since his father's death, Martin had been removed from his familiar surroundings, including his beloved church, where he sang in the choir. After coming to the nursing home, Martin became belligerent and uncooperative with the staff and medical personnel.

Sacks soon learned that Martin was the son of a famous Metropolitan Opera musician and had enjoyed a very close relationship with his father. Martin had attended every performance at the Met with his father. Martin's father sometimes placed him in the back row of the chorus, even though his son couldn't sing very well. However, Martin loved to sing. He had memorized *Grove's Dictionary of Music and Musicians,* and the librettos of more than two thousand operas.

One day during a diagnostic session with Sacks, Martin suddenly shouted, "I have to sing. I can't live without it. I can't pray without my music." Then he looked Sacks directly in the eyes and quietly said, "Music was to Bach the apparatus of worship. From *Grove's* article on Bach, page 304."

After this surprising outburst, Sacks arranged for Martin to go back to his old church and sing again with the choir. Sacks recalled that when Martin sang, he stood tall and straight, with absolutely no sign of his Parkinson's disease.

Martin seemed to feel the music down to the depths of his soul. Back in his old role in the church choir, Martin became a changed man. He was now warm and friendly with everyone at the home. Martin got his music and his groove back.

We Boomers have also felt a sense of freedom and liberation through music, as we moved and gyrated our bodies to rock, Motown, or country swing beats. Yet it seems that many of us have become "unmusicked." The dullness of the mainstream culture, the responsibilities of parenting and midlife, and the prospects of retirement have fulfilled the prophecy of the words from a popular song, "The Day the Music Died." In ReFirement we desperately need to get our music back.

In the envelope-pushing TV series, *Alley McBeal,* a number of major characters hear their own personal music at very strange times during their work lives. When those music tapes begin, the TV characters fall into a kinetic-like trance and begin to move to their own personal song. By having the show's characters suddenly break into movement in courtrooms or in elevators or just on the street, the writers are urging each of us to find the music within ourselves and not be afraid to move to it, even in public.

Recently I attended a "Retro-Beatles" concert in Minneapolis performed by a fantastic group of Liverpool impersonators from Ohio. The median age of the audience was well over forty-five. When the first song was played, I watched hundreds of women spontaneously rise from their Orchestra Hall seats and effortlessly move their bodies, smiling to the pulsating rhythms of the songs we all know by heart. Three women high above me in the third balcony seemed to be dancing suspended in midair. A few men tried to match their spontaneity and style, but it was the women in the audience who were able to immediately respond to the music, forget where they were, and just go wherever the beat took them!

Activities to **ReFire** your life

Using Music to ReFire

Think back through your life. What role did music play?

> Age 1–10
> 11–20
> 21–30
> 31–40
> 41–50
> 51–now

List ways you might use music to get your groove back. Here are some ideas to get you started:

- Listen to a tape or CD of music you loved when you were in your teens or twenties.
- Get out your old instrument, or begin lessons on an instrument you've always dreamed of playing.
- Sing in a community chorus or church choir.
- Listen to a type of music you've never heard before.
- Go to a concert, recital, or club with live music.
- Sometime during the next week or two discuss the role of music in your life with a teenager or twenty-something and with an elder. Compare notes.

Humor

Like music, humor is also a hallmark of our generation. From childhood to young adulthood, we were raised on comic greats such as the Three Stooges, Milton Berle, Bob Hope, Lucille Ball, Dean Martin and Jerry Lewis, Red Skelton, Lily Tomlin and *Laugh In,* Carol Burnett, the Smothers Brothers, Bob Newhart, and *Saturday Night Live's* "Not Ready for Prime Time Players." Now we take ourselves far too seriously. This is why the younger generations tell us "to lighten up" or to "get a life"! In our continuing search for perfection and achievement, we have left an important asset behind—our humor.

Besides being a balancing force to counteract self-righteousness, pomposity, and the steady stream of depressing stories coming daily from the media, humor is also essential to creating a healthy lifestyle.

If you build a positive focus in your life, you reduce stress and support your body's ability to fight disease. Some of the key positive attitudes that are helpful to the immune system are love, hope, optimism, caring, intimacy, joy, and laughter. Building more humor into your life helps releases endorphins and neuropeptides throughout your body. As Groucho Marx said, "A clown is like an aspirin—only he works twice as fast."

"If you build a positive focus in your life, you reduce stress and support your body's ability to fight disease."

Bernie Siegel, medical doctor and author, has studied the relationship of humor to health. He says, "Given all the evidence that watching a humorous video strengthens different components of our immune system, it makes sense that individuals who have a better developed sense of humor" [meaning that they find more humor in their everyday lives] "seek out humor more often and laugh more—should have a stronger immune system. . . . The simple truth is that happy people generally don't get sick."

Norman Cousins was the editor of the prestigious literary journal, the *Saturday Review*. He was diagnosed with an incurable disease of the connecting tissue that binds body cells together. The disease caused him to be in excruciating pain every moment of his life. The prognosis was that the pain would only get worse, leading to an early death. Cousins, not wanting to be continually medicated and dulled with pain killers, asked to be moved from his hospital bed to an apartment room near the hospital. He had remembered reading in a medical study that negative emotions directly affect the adrenal glands. He thought if this were true, perhaps positive emotions (encouraged by humor and laughter) would work to positively affect his body.

Cousins spent the next several weeks and months on a steady diet of high doses of vitamin C, *Candid Camera* films, and his nurse reading aloud to him from White's *Subtreasury of American Humor*. He discovered that a two-hour period of laughter allowed him to sleep pain free for four hours. In a matter of months, the "incurable disease" completely disappeared. Cousins quit his job at the *Saturday Review*, ReFired, and joined the faculty at UCLA's medical school, where he formed a humor and medicine task force.

Laugh at Yourself

A good sense of humor means being able to laugh at oneself. Recall your week. Think of some mistakes you have made or circumstances in which you have felt very resistant. Try to find a funny angle on what happened.

When you are able to smile knowingly at your own foibles, your life will take on a lightness you've not know before. You will find it easier to forgive yourself for your failures and missteps. Self-forgiveness frees up a lot of physical and psychic energy to use elsewhere. Start to expect humor in your life! This will pave the way for deeper belonging and greater risk taking.

Try reading one humorous book during the next six months. Or check out some funny videos from the library or video store.

Adventure

During the next thirty to forty years, we can increase our ability to see life as a generational and personal adventure. Life can be a journey open to new dreams, new possibilities, and new opportunities. Young people will be looking to us as elders to give them guidance for their lives by sharing our wisdom and experience. To do this, we must stay current and involved with the present and not withdraw, as so many older people are doing today.

Lyn, born in 1946, is one of the oldest Baby Boomers. For years she had gladly watched her husband and teenage son go off camping in northern Minnesota and Wisconsin, grateful for their good relationship and happy to let them do their "guy thing." But when her son was about to celebrate his twenty-first birthday, and father and son were planning a backpacking trip to the Upper Peninsula in Michigan, Lyn decided she wanted to share in the adventure.

She had some self-doubts. They would have to carry all their equipment and food for five days. There would be no showers. They'd have to purify water from the lake for cooking and drinking. There would be bears. Would she be able to keep up the pace? Would she enjoy it? The vision of herself sitting on the shores of Lake Superior was enough to overcome any of her misgivings.

In the succeeding days, Lyn found she loved cooking on the small camp stove, watching the sun set over Lake Superior, hiking along the cliffs at the top of the Painted Rocks, discovering mushrooms she had never seen before, sitting around the campfire at night while her son, a biology major, read aloud from *Vegetation of Wisconsin,* and even bathing in the icy waters of the lake. One afternoon she enjoyed several hours of solitude while her husband and son set off for an eight-mile hike.

Lyn discovered—as did her husband and son—that she could keep up, and that she loved backpacking and camping. And all the next winter she was thinking of new places to camp when summer rolled around.

Lyn took a risk and found a new adventure that will continue to enrich her life. From Lyn's story we can learn that if we are afraid to begin the hike, we will never find what's on the trail.

Many of my friends tell me that seeing your life as an adventure seems to be easier if you have a partner or, like Lyn, a family to share your adventure journey. Many single Boomers talk about having fewer friends today than they did twenty years ago. And they lament on how difficult it is to make new friends. One of the important challenges of ReFirement is to help all individuals of all ages—single, divorced, and widowed—create the "life adventure" support systems they need to get their groove back.

Make Your Life an Adventure

Plan small adventures for yourself. Take a different route to work. Do something your friends would say, "That just isn't like her." Make a list of the things you would like to do but don't think that you can—then figure out a way to do them.

Plan one big adventure. This might require a three-, five-, or ten-year plan. Just make sure that it will be a big adventure for you.

Pushing Your Envelope

On my forty-fifth birthday, I decided that during every year to come I would do something that I had never done before. I didn't care if I became an expert or not or even whether I continued the activity for an ongoing period of time. I intended only to begin to test my limits and "push my own envelope." Since that birthday, I have done the following:

- Took lessons in order to play one blues song on the piano, even though I don't read music.

- Delivered a stand-up comedy routine on an "open mike" stage.

- Talked each week in some depth with a person from one of the other four living generations.

- Relearned how to pray and started reading the Bible more regularly.

- Switched my golf game from the right side to both the right and left sides (long woods and irons with my left hand and my short game from the right side). I had never played any sport left-handed before.

Music, humor, life adventure, and pushing your own envelope can help you get your groove back and change your life. The more you incorporate these things into your daily life, the more interesting and healthier you will become. Once you have your groove back, you will be in a much better place, psychologically and physically, to begin your ReFirement planning.

Push Your Envelope Now!

Make a list of a half dozen activities you believed you were not capable of doing or were never interested in doing. (Let's keep this legal!) Over the next six months, do one or more of them. For instance:

- Study a subject that has always interested you, and write a report as you did in school.
- Blindfold yourself and see how much you can accomplish at home.
- Try walking backward for part of a day. (It's up to you if you want to do this in public!)
- Attend an event that you never thought you would enjoy, but go with an open mind.
- Eat something you have never eaten or buy something different to wear that you always wished you had the nerve to wear before.
- If you are right-handed, use your left hand for a few hours, or vice versa.

After you have done a few of the things on your list, you will start getting in the habit of experimenting with moving beyond your cozy, comfort zone. You will have risked pushing your personal envelope. Each time you do this, it becomes easier. Later, when life gives you no choice but to move out of your familiar ways of being and doing, you will be much more prepared for positively accepting change.

Chapter 5

Taking Charge of Your Own Health

We are the first generation in human history that can expect to live twenty to thirty years after age sixty-five as healthy, energetic, productive, and creative people. One of the highest predictors of good health is more education, and we are the most educated of all the generations living today. This longevity, coupled with our numbers, will present us with a chance to dramatically change the way we look at health and health care in our country.

Improving the health of all Americans begins with a deep and profound personal commitment by every one of us to create healthy, respectful, caring, and cooperative communities. In these ReFirement communities:

- Individuals of all ages will take more personal responsibility for their own health.

- People of all ages will be encouraged to use their gifts regardless of age, or develop new ones, to help others.

- Quality care in *all* forms will be creatively provided when it is needed.

- Alternative and preventive approaches will be emphasized along with more traditional "scientific" medical care.

- Everyone will have an opportunity to participate in positive social networks.
- These healthy communities will recognize the obvious connections between illness and the kind of air we breath, the water we drink, and the food we consume.

It will be a great disappointment if we are unable to fulfill all of the possibilities of our own ReFirement because of health problems that are largely preventable. Fortunately, our scientific understanding of health, and even aging, is changing rapidly. Our generation is leading the way in helping shift the paradigm from an approach to health based primarily on how we treat disease to a more holistic wellness model that shows us how to prevent illness and become more healthy and energetic.

Use It Or Lose It! A ReFirement Mantra

The CBS news magazine *48 Hours* aired an hour-long special on aging and health. Two of the most important segments dealt with current research on the brain and the story of an 102-year-old practicing woman doctor.

The brain research report included detailed scans of frontal lobes from the brains of a twenty-one year old and an eighty year old. You could clearly see differences. The color red represented signs of activity in the twenty-one year old's scan. We learned this young person was active, going to college, and generally optimistic. But the eighty year old's scan was completely gray—no color. This person was more sedentary, alone, and not very involved in life in spite of no major illnesses. The exciting news came when the researcher said she had many other brain scans of older people that looked identical to those of younger people. These older people—we could call them ReFirement pioneers—were using their brains and their bodies, and the scans of their activity levels showed that. "We believe in the 'use it or lose it' approach to mental health and aging," the researcher said.

48 Hours also introduced us to a woman who received her medical degree in 1928 and is still practicing pediatric medicine at the age of 102. This woman walks almost two miles every day, keeps up with medical journals and new advances in drugs and technology, and eats a well-balanced diet. She loves her work and has never even considered retiring. When the reporter asked her how long she would keep practicing medicine, she said, "When I can't help these children anymore, I will quit." Now that's a positive ReFirement mentality!

Creating Your Own Wellness Plan

The concept of ReFirement does not accept anything as inevitable except death. Once we turn the idea of aging upside down, our own personal health should become our first priority. The following suggestions make up a ReFirement prescription for how to start today and stay healthy for the rest of your life.

1. **Make physical fitness part of your personal wellness plan.**
   The Boomer generation was responsible for creating the physical-fitness movement in this country. For years, infomercials have sold us new exercise equipment, tapes, and videos. (In fact, these pitches were so successful that they spawned a secondary

industry to sell used exercise equipment.) But for many us, increasingly hectic schedules got in the way of our good intentions about exercise. In addition, the infomercial promises did not seem to be fulfilled as magically as we had hoped. But I think that the biggest reason for the decline in exercise and the increase in sedentary lifestyles is because our reasons for getting trim were not right. Most of us wanted to shed our extra five, ten, or twenty pounds in order to look more attractive—not because we wanted to become more healthy! By letting go of our vain visions of self, we have an opportunity to age more successfully and become more holistic about our health.

Activities to ReFire your life

Simple Physical Exercises

During this week, use your body to move yourself around. Try bypassing the escalator or elevator and use the stairs—if only for a few floors. Walk or bike to a neighborhood store or restaurant. Buy a set of light weights. After thirty days, note how you have incorporated more healthful movement into your life. Keep looking for opportunities to use your physical abilities to move yourself around.

2. **Pay attention to *all* parts of your body.**

   For example, let's talk feet. Today, there are 147 podiatrists and podiatry clinics listed in the Miami-area *Yellow Pages*—and these are just the specialists! It is clear that older generations have not treated, or have not had the luxury of treating, their feet with great care. Their shoes, women's in particular, were often not primarily designed for comfort and foot health. For decades women were expected, and encouraged by the moguls of fashion, to work in high heels, causing painful damage to their feet. Today, the new fashions for women feature even higher heels than ever.

   Men and women should be able to wear attractive but more comfortable lower-heeled shoes and not be embarrassed to seek out orthopedic inserts when needed. We should also feel encouraged to enjoy foot massages. A preventive approach to Boomer foot care will serve us well in our elder years.

3. **Take advantage of free or low-cost prevention and wellness care.**

   A holistic approach to our general health care need not be expensive. In fact much of what we can do through our own self-care will be entirely free! Remember the health benefits of laughter:

   - Increases antibodies that combat respiratory disease

   - Decreases serum cortisol which provides an antidote for the harmful effects of stress

   - Secretes an enzyme that tends to protect the stomach from ulcers

- Conditions our abdominal muscles
- Reduces heart rate and blood pressure
- Liberates our natural immune boosters
- Increases our endorphins—the body's natural pain reliever

In fact, laughter is considered so powerful that the Mbuti hunter-gathers of northeast Zaire use humor and laughter to dissipate intertribal quarrels! Laughter comes at no cost to us. It is a natural gift to which we all have access. We can treat ourselves to it anytime!

You might also consider walking. Every fitness book or exercise guru agrees on the benefits of walking at least twenty minutes a day. Walking is helpful for the cardiovascular system, aids in digestion, releases good endorphins, and allows you to enjoy every season of nature's wonders. In fact, an 80-year-old walker gave me an invaluable tip for depression: If you walk outside with your head held high and your eyes forward, you will get a break from whatever is bringing you down. Try it.

You could also try organic gardening. The rewards you receive for caring, nurturing, and loving your plants are a benefit in themselves. Gardening is a good exercise which keeps on giving during the harvest. Like laughing and walking, gardening can be a relatively inexpensive and a great way to exercise personal control over your own health.

4. **Make your prevention and wellness plan simple.** Many of us take our health for granted until we receive a midlife "wake-up" call—in the form of an

illness. I recently talked with a woman who enjoyed good health for her entire life. She loved the outdoors and spent a great deal of time in outdoor adventure and recreation. It was not until a surprising illness struck her that she finally realized how much she had taken her health for granted. She realized at last that she must take time from her increasingly stressful professional life and begin to focus more of her attention on healthy self-care. Acknowledging that she already had some good habits, such as regular walking, she decided to add several new prevention methods to her life—a better-balanced diet, regular stretching and weightlifting, breathing exercises, and meditation. At last she began to understand that self-care practices were not an add-on to her "to do" list. Rather they were an essential part of her daily lifestyle.

We are more likely to stick to new preventive health measures if we keep it simple, gradually adding techniques and adapting them to fit our lifestyles and improve our ongoing health. Here are a few concrete, simple ideas for improving our health. Reflect on your current methods of practicing wellness. Then, at your own pace, incorporate the new items you wish to try from this list. Try them out slowly. The key is to make your health a natural part of your daily lifestyle.

"We are more likely to stick to new preventive health measures if we keep it simple. . ."

Diet

- Add more fiber to your meals by eating more fruits, vegetables, and whole grains.

- Consider using more organic food. It sometimes costs a bit more but helps us avoid potentially damaging chemicals and questionable irradiation. (As with questions about health information, the jury is still out on what truly is healthfully produced food. My belief is to eat food that has had as little human manipulation as possible.)

- Eat balanced meals and avoid saturated fats.

Activities to ReFire *your life*

Mindless & Mindful Food Choices

For a few days, write down exactly what you eat. Don't think of this list as a calorie list. Just list the type of food. Next time you go grocery shopping, deliberately reach for fresh and organic foods in place of the processed food you may have been eating. Make conscious exchanges of "mindless" food for "mindful" food.

Exercise and muscle tone

One of the facts of aging is that the muscles are one one of the first parts of our body to lose strength and tone. You want the strongest muscles possible as you age.

- Do muscle stretches. An experienced physical therapist or exercise coach can help you get started on simple routines.

- Lift weights to keep muscle tone or build new muscle. Remember, you don't have to be a *muscle builder.* Keep it simple.

- Walk whenever you can—across the parking lot, up the stairs. Keep your legs healthy by using them!

Other special body care

- Protect your skin from the sun.

- Treat your skin to regular moisturizing.

- Increase awareness of your posture and be attentive to walking and sitting upright. This may mean choosing office and home furniture that is more supportive of your back. You can also find videos to instruct you on how to achieve proper, healthy posture.

- Wear comfortable and supportive footwear.

- Schedule an annual comprehensive physical exam with your physician. Insist on all appropriate tests based on your age and family history.

Stress reducers

- Get a periodic massage.

- Practice breathing techniques

- Schedule time for yourself. Reflect, meditate, pray, enjoy nature. Plan regular breaks from your busy and stressful daily routine.

- Take your scheduled vacation time.

- Don't feel guilty about taking personal time or a weekend for yourself.

- Adopt a pet.

Give Yourself a Treat

Treat yourself this week! Get a full body massage, take a bubble bath, take a walk in a beautiful park, or just look at nature from a bench or a scenic overlook. Schedule a couple days of retreat time just for you.

5. Get more balance in your life.

The ancient Greeks told us a long time ago, "In the middle stands virtue."

When you talk to Baby Boomers, listen to them discuss the concept of balance in their lives. You'll probably hear one of the following statements:

"I'm too busy to take time for myself."

"I'm worried I don't have enough in my 401k to retire as soon as I want."

"I'm staying in this job because I'm helping my children get through college or graduate school."

"Life is getting so fast I just can't ever seem to catch up."

Many of us are running so fast that we have forgotten why we even started the race.

When any living system on this planet is pushed to extremes, it is unhealthy. Any ecosystem will have a hard time surviving if it is forced to deal with extreme conditions over an extended period of time. In fact, almost every major human and environmental calamity of the past centuries occurred when extremes became the norm and moderation was forgotten. Yet, we continue to subject ourselves to extended periods of bad nutrition, overwork, insufficient rest, continuing stress, and a lack of loving human touch and physical warmth. It is no wonder there is a multibillion dollar pharmaceutical and psychiatric industry that supplies legal and expensive drugs to try and keep distressed individuals in an altered state of euphoria and equilibrium. ReFiring Boomers have an opportunity to change all this and put their physical, intellectual, and emotional lives into better balance.

In 1976, I visited the People's Republic of China. The group I traveled with was trying to understand how the Chinese achieved a grass roots education on a variety of important issues like health care and prevention. When I saw my first health clinic out in the remote countryside, I learned one Chinese notion of balance in health care. The little clinic was nothing more than a one-room brick building with a few windows and a front door. Inside, the clinic room was sparse and clean. A steel examination table stood in the middle of the room, and flanking it on both sides against the rear wall, were two small tables.

We asked the local "barefoot doctor" (not a physician, but a young woman trained to help the Chinese peasants take control of their own health planning) why there were two tables near the back wall. She explained that Western medicine was largely built on treating individual trauma. Western physicians see an illness and try to cure it. The Western physician is most powerful because he or she has the most knowledge. In that system, the patient is more passive and relies on the doctor. The Chinese health care worker said that the Chinese medical system was built on the concept of prevention—to promote wellness as well as help people who are sick. The young woman said she tries to get everybody of all ages in the village to understand the fact that disease threatens us when our bodies are most vulnerable. The healthier we stay in mind and body, the less chance we will face illness. She then told us about the two tables.

The table to the left was the Western medicine table. We saw an assortment of prescription drugs, medications, and other diagnostic tools used in the West. The table to the right was the traditional Chinese medicine table. It contained acupuncture needles, local herbs, teas, and other natural remedies that help prevent or heal illness by strengthening the body's natural immune system. She explained that the Chinese try to balance the best of both medical approaches so they will complement each another and that was why both were in the same room.

We can learn a great deal from the Chinese about how to incorporate the concept of balance in our lives. One simple part of this principle is to always seek moderation—or the middle way. When you feel you are moving towards an extreme, back away and remember the proverb, "In the middle stands virtue."

"When you feel you are moving towards an extreme, back away and remember the proverb, 'In the middle stands virtue.'"

6. **Be open to alternatives in medicine and care.**
   Boomers have had the advantages of some of the advances made by Western biomedicine—the kind we experience when we go to our M.D. or medical clinic or hospital. Our families have had the blessings of vaccines against infectious diseases like polio, transplant technology, new treatments for cancer, the advent of bionic joints, and the spectacular mapping of the entire human genome.

   This kind of hi-tech Western biomedicine is wonderful for treating many kinds of diseases—especially infectious diseases and accidental traumas. It is often, however, less good at diagnosing and treating chronic conditions like fibromyalgia or arthritis that do not yield to a quick fix.

   For these reasons many Boomers—and others—are turning to various forms of "alternative" medicine. These medical practices include such disparate modalities as chiropractic, naturopathy, homeopathy, massage, acupuncture, prayer, herbal remedies, aroma therapy, shamanism, and Native American medicine. According to the *New England Journal of Medicine,* nearly one-third of Americans

have used some form of alternative medical care—
and the numbers are growing.

We enjoy a much wider range of choices in wellness and healing than did our parents, and this
appeals to our Boomer values of experimentation
and risk taking. This also means we have to make
tough choices about the form of medicine to seek.
We need what Ernest Hemingway called a good
"crap detector." Boomers now have the unique
opportunity to make use
of a wide variety of
healing approaches—
old and new, Eastern
and Western, alternative
and mainstream—to
seek greater health and
wholeness.

> *"Boomers now have
> the unique opportu-
> nity to make use of a
> wide variety of healing
> approaches . . . to seek
> greater health and
> wholeness."*

7. **Be aware that your health is directly related to your
   environment.**
   You have probably read in the popular press that our
   generation will be living longer and healthier lives.
   Yet one of the challenging unknowns for the Boomer
   generation is that, beginning in our childhood, we
   were exposed to numerous chemicals and pollutants
   with unknown effects over a long period of exposure.
   These included food additives and preservatives,
   food dyes and coloring, exhaust emissions, and
   more recently, irradiation of our foods. In addition,
   as children many of us may have been exposed to a
   great deal more than normal background radiation
   due to nuclear fallout from military and industrial
   experiments and as a result of severe pollution in

urban areas. The evidence of our damaged health resulting from exposure to such chemicals and pollutants may not show up until our sixties or seventies. While Boomers should not obsess about the potential serious outcomes of these unseen dangers from our past, we must be aware of, and concerned about, what might improve our immune systems and the general state of our health.

Learning from a ReFirement pioneer

Vilma Vitanza, age seventy-one, from Oakland, California, was born in Honduras. Like many Hondurans, she worked for the United Fruit Company. She served as a lab assistant for scientists who were researching fungi and bacterial diseases of bananas. This work brought her into direct contact with dangerous chemicals, including pesticides that are heavily used on banana crops.

Divorced at the age thirty-five, Vilma discovered there was no room for advancement at United Fruit. In 1967 she emigrated with her family and secured a job at the University of California at Berkeley as a lab technician. She remained in this position for the next eighteen years. During this time, she was exposed to the residual gases of pesticides and to lacrylamide—a dangerous neurotoxin.

Vilma began having symptoms of irritability, skin rashes, and allergies. When she went to the doctors, they dismissed her complaints and told her it was due to menopause. Then, she began to get severe pains in her joints that would some-times cause her to collapse in the lab. She started experiencing paranoia. Finally, she suffered a complete collapse of her immune system. At that point, the university health care system secured a psychiatrist, a neuropsychologist, an immunologist, and an environmental illness specialist to treat her. But things got even worse. Vilma forgot how to spell, developed three new personalities, had severe memory problems, and lost her sense of humor. At the age of fifty-six, she became suicidal and avoided even people she knew, because she felt ashamed. It was, she says, as if both her brain and mind had been raped.

Eventually Vilma started to recover physically. She began to get her groove back. Vilma saw an ad for StAGEbridge Theater in Oakland, California, a theater company dedicated to bringing the young and old together. It was here that Vilma found a way to express herself without being laughed at or judged. Through structured exercises with the theater group, she was able to focus and make her senses work together. She retaught herself how to read, and she began auditing classes at San Francisco State University. Her mind began to respond, and her self-image began to improve. Vilma auditioned for plays and went to schools to perform for kids. She says she was like a child herself because she was dependent on so many people for help. In 1989, she laughed for the first time in years. This is when she realized she was on the road to recovery.

She is now trying to find out now why she is here in this world and what she has to contribute based on her troubled life journey. Vilma knows real fear—physical and mental— and how frightening it can be to have your life dramatically change. She also knows that, at the age of seventy-one, she enjoys the greatest freedom she has ever had. She wants to learn more about how to use that freedom to give herself totally to her theater audiences. She is trying to reach the honesty and truth that is within her. Vilma says, "If we are able to lose our egos and become more humble, we can develop better relationships with each other. This search for truth is what will keep me alive."

Instead of escaping into a denial of our aging, we are better served by claiming responsibility now for maintaining a healthy and thriving environment as we age. ReFired men and women need to ask themselves a simple question: Are we willing to get involved in helping to pass on an environment to future generations better than the one we received?

Activities to ReFire your life

Easy Steps to Preventive Health

Take a few minutes this week and assess your current preventive health practices. Give yourself some credit for the prevention you are already doing. Which ones have you added to your daily life in the past months and years? For example:

- getting more fresh air
- finding new scents and aromas in nature
- cooking with more herbs and natural ingredients
- dancing

Then select two or three new ones and add them to your current practices.

What is the one most important change you could make in your present health care? What prevents you from making it? What would help you make it?

Chapter 6

Men Are from Mars. Women Are from Venus.

But We Both Live on Earth!

We begin the twenty-first century with an incredible opportunity to improve relationships between men and women in America. We know there are significant differences. After all, men are from Mars and women are from Venus! In ReFirement however, both genders will need to work together to eliminate gender inequalities and other forms of discrimination wherever they exist. And both men and women will benefit by seeking to understand each others' potentials, fears, and opportunities in an aging society.

As a generation raised on the values of entitlement and high expectations, we often dismiss the amazing progress we have made over the past forty years. For example, as a result of the women's movement, tremendous gains have been made in breaking down stereotypical roles in the workplace, the military, and the family. Look at attitudes today compared to 1960 regarding sexual harassment, participation by women and girls in competitive sports, and in business leadership. Yes, women have made strong gains, but we all have a long way to go before we can talk seriously about equality.

While men still wield considerably more economic and political power, we have trouble overcoming competitive feelings and finding real friendships with each other. We lack personal support systems. Many of us are unable to find satisfaction or happiness in our jobs. We suffer from stress and depression that helps shorten our lifespans by ten to fifteen years compared to women. Plus some males today may also experience "reverse discrimination." I hear many stories about men applying for jobs and hearing this refrain: "As a white male, your chances for getting that job are absolutely zip!"

The Challenges for Boomer Women

Before we examine how ReFirement can guide this generation to a better resolution of the so-called "battle of the sexes," it is important to identify the special needs and challenges women in their forties and fifties will face if the current retirement system continues.

A female colleague of mine tells me that financial well-being is a hot topic among her friends. Their discussion varies from hopeful optimism among the married women to anxious and cynical comments among those—including herself—who are divorced. Her friends are bright women— some with college education and others with advanced graduate degrees. All are creative, engaged in meaningful work that serves important societal needs. Some are self-employed, while others work for employers. My colleague says the married women often talk of traveling, spending part of the year in warmer climates, and urging their husbands to leave jobs that have become increasingly stress-producing as down-sizing has occurred all around them.

However, the single women in this group of friends say straight out that because of financial needs they will never be able to quit working. Retirement is not even a word in their vocabulary, and they wonder how many years past age sixty-two they will need to remain employed. Nearly all these single, divorced women admit to meager or nearly nonexistent financial portfolios, and no pensions. Some admit they gasped when they read the estimate of the meager Social Security payments for which they will be eligible at age sixty-two, sixty-five, or seventy. A few of these women say that, to maintain their current sanity they try not to think about their elder years at all.

On the other hand, many of these same women also say that they plan to work at least part-time in their elder years because they want to continue to express themselves creatively through their work and to continue to make significant contributions to society. So whether they will work to survive economically or to survive emotionally, traditional retirement is not a goal for many Boomer women. I believe that ReFirement is a much more appropriate banner under which they can gather.

In ReFirement, Boomer women from all races and cultures will face special issues. The statistics may seem ironic or even contradictory. Ten million American households are currently headed by women. More than half the work force is made up of women, and women participate in over eighty-five percent of all savings and investment decisions in this economy.

On the other hand, women make only sixty percent of what men make doing comparable work. And, on average, women take off about ten years from their working life to care for children. Moreover, Boomer women have suffered financially from high rates of divorce, spousal neglect or abuse, and a scandalous child support system. Even those who have moved into corporate work settings have frequently faced the financial barriers caused by glass ceilings.

It is clear that traditional retirement, designed primarily for men, cannot possibly meet the needs of millions of aging Boomer women. Nancy Dailey in her book *When Baby Boomer Women Retire*, a pioneering research study, notes that fewer than twenty percent of these women can reliably feel financially secure about their elder years. She writes:

> *"It is clear that traditional retirement, designed primarily for men, cannot possibly meet the needs of millions of aging Boomer women."*

Baby Boom women who are married, possess a college degree, receive high earnings, and own a home can expect to experience a comfortable retirement. Yet, even these women may face economic jeopardy since risk factors such as divorce or loss of a job could reduce their future prospects. Marriage, education, occupation, and home ownership—these are the variables that best predict the future for Baby Boom women. Possession of all four variables indicate high retirement security; absence of any one of the variables increases the risk of poverty in old age.

Dailey's extensive research reveals several important findings:

1. Boomer women's elder years will be unlike male
   patterns.
2. Traditional sources of retirement income such as
   Social Security, pensions, and personal savings will
   be insufficient for most Boomer women.
3. Boomer women will enter their elder years as family
   caretakers for the country's elderly.

Women are expected to outlive their male counterparts by
anywhere from eight to fifteen years. That longevity fact
alone will negatively impact their retirement scenarios. In
addition, women's employment patterns (such as lower
wages than men for comparable work and years out of the
workforce or working part-time while raising children) will
limit both Social Security and pensions as well as savings for
their elder years.

Single mothers have often forsaken savings for immediate needs related to home and family. Although many
women may be planning to work full-time during much of
their sixties, and part-time thereafter, Dailey's study also
reminds us that ageism in employment will likely affect
them. Unless there are major changes in employment
patterns, women, as they grow older, will not find it easy to
keep good jobs.

Boomer women are often advised to start serious financial planning right now—at whatever age they are. The
reality is that thirty-seven million women of all ages are
already investing and control six trillion dollars of investment. And they tend to do 1.4 percent better as investors
than men.

Boomer women should not fall into the trap of focusing almost exclusively on the need for financial resources in their older years. If they do, they will forget to identify the many personal assets they bring to their ReFirement. A higher percentage than ever before have college educations and even advanced degrees. Millions have held challenging positions in employment, some creating and running their own businesses. Right now more women than men are starting businesses, and they are becoming major players in E-commerce and information technology. This means they bring considerable new skills and knowledge to ReFirement. The increasing equity in gender roles will result in producing aging women with unparalleled savvy and confidence as well as greater creative freedom to design new work and roles utilizing developing technology.

> *"The increasing equity in gender roles will result in producing aging women with unparalleled savvy and confidence as well as greater creative freedom to design new work and roles utilizing developing technology."*

Perhaps Boomer women should say honestly what their fears and concerns are—to name them out loud. Share the "unedited version" with friends or other trusted persons who are not necessarily financial gurus. Giving voice to retirement fears is a huge and freeing step for Boomers as they begin to ReFire.

The next step may be to speak about these same fears and realities with someone who has financial and life-planning expertise. (This step may be easier when they have first broken through their personal denial and voiced fears and realities with friends or trusted colleagues who are not experts.)

Another colleague of mine told me she believed for years that she could not afford to visit a financial planner. Finally at about age fifty, she built up her courage, compiled a list of her basic financial assets and liabilities and made an appointment. She quickly found herself hugely embarrassed when the planner looked over her paperwork, turned to her and said: "Well, clearly you have absolutely nothing! But if you keep working on it over the next few years, you may find you can pay off your debt and then start having fun investing." She walked out reeling with his suggestions of enormously increasing her deductibles on insurance, not even considering disability insurance even though she was self-employed, and other initiatives she should or should not take. But mostly she remembered that the visit had been one of the most shaming experiences of her life.

Clearly the choice of financial planner/advisor must have more than one dimension. The coming years will create a much greater demand for life planning professionals who have not only financial expertise but some psychological understanding of what is going on with their clients and the ability to assist them in identifying their total human capital portfolio.

Keep in mind, however, the considerable strides Boomer women have made toward financial security. Sixty-two percent of all women already seek professional financial investment help, and approximately 55,000 women currently work in the financial security business. Whether married or single, women are increasingly seeking out financial and life planning advice and becoming more sophisticated in managing their own lives and money.

What the Genders Share in Common

Let's state flat out what Boomer men and women have in common. Both will face age discrimination connected to a retirement system in which few are valued after they reach a certain age. I have a refrigerator magnet that says, "If you don't think age discrimination affects you, just wait awhile." When we join together to replace retirement with ReFirement, there is real hope for ending one of our most pernicious and neglected forms of discrimination.

> *"If you don't think age discrimination affects you, just wait awhile."*

For most of their lives, women have been the objects of marketing that encourages them to look young. Today, as we saw in the chapter, "Turning Aging Upside Down," men are the emerging market for the billion dollar cosmetic, pharmaceutical, and elective plastic surgery industries. The advertising that objectifies men and women plays on our vanity and ultimately undermines our self-concept. Both men and women need to support each other and find better ways to accept their own aging and wisely use their discretionary incomes.

Both genders need to work together in order to ensure that the economic, social, and political tenets of ReFirement succeed. If cooperation is lacking between genders and among generations, real changes enabling all ages to fully develop their talents and skills with dignity will be difficult to achieve. By collaborating with both older and younger generations, Boomers will eventually secure the political power and leadership needed to make major changes in public policies affecting people's elder years and how they impact other generations.

ReFirement: The Perfect Platform for Relationship Changes

Author Susan Faludi, the best-selling feminist author who first explored men's resistance to the progress of women, is now publishing new research on male identity. Her research documents a comparable situation among men who struggle with loss and identity as the traditional views and codes about manhood are no longer honored. Although women had the initial advantage of many social movements, namely a definable oppressor, men are largely unable to start a comparable revolution because their enemy is largely unidentifiable. Faced with massive down-sizing and job insecurities in a transitional global economy, changing expectations of a man's role in the family and within larger society, and continuing pressure to act in control of their lives and emotions—even when it is increasingly clear that their lives are often out of control and their social role is increasingly unclear—men have no clear enemies or oppressors. Instead, they are still often seen as the oppressors yet feel trapped in systems in ways both distinct yet similar to the entrapment women experience.

Faludi affirms the necessity of both women and men to work together to create a new paradigm that will allow both sexes to seek greater human freedom and opportunities to serve humanity. *ReFirement is that paradigm.* It begins when men and women of our generation recognize our common values: belonging, entitlement, giving back, high expectations, experimentation, and risk-taking. Boomers—both women and men—are indeed entitled to personal freedom for expressing their authentic selves in their ReFirement years, free of old societal pressures. A historic opportunity exists to understand each other's journeys and to quit

blaming each other. Both genders can gain by offering and
receiving forgiveness and forging a common effort. A deeper
level of belonging to the human family is bound to emerge
from such a mutuality. Moreover, it will open all kinds of
possibilities for future generations as well, thus offering a
great gift to all.

It comes down to respecting, caring, and cooperating
with one another. The relationships between men and
women are primary relationships in the family, the workplace, and in the community. If we put our energy and belief
in the possibilities of ReFirement, we can create a new
society based on a very different set of values than we experience today. It is very clear we will not be able to achieve the
depth and quality of change required by ReFirement if we
work at it separately. I believe and hope we are finally ready
to work together.

Activities to ReFire your life

What Are the Gender Problems?

What do you see as the biggest problems that exist
between the genders today? How would the
ReFirement ideas you've read in this book help solve
these problems?

Reaching Common Ground

Initiate a conversation with a family member, friend, or colleague of the opposite gender about how men and women might seek greater mutual understanding and cooperation as they prepare for their elder years. Identify some concrete steps and methods. Envision together several possible outcomes of such mutuality. Share your personal hopes for such a cooperative approach in ReFirement.

In the coming month, talk with one male and one female from a younger generation and one male and female from an older generation about gender issues. Ask them to name the issues they think are most important.

Ask a man and a woman of an older generation and a man and woman of a younger generation how they would go about building cooperation between the genders—collaboration that would lead to greater freedom and possibilities for both and result in more service to humanity as a whole.

Chapter 7

Changing Through Healing and Forgiveness

A good first step to understand the range of diversity in our society is to recognize the diversity of our own generation. Of the 76 million Baby Boomers born in the United States, 18 million come from non-Caucasian backgrounds: 9.5 million are African Americans; 6.1 million Latinos; and about 2.8 million represent other minorities. The remaining 58 million Caucasians are ethnically and culturally diverse. And the United States is rapidly becoming even more diverse.

A major ReFirement challenge is to see our growing diversity as a great gift and opportunity rather than an insurmountable problem. The new ReFirement mindset of transformation, renewal, and pushing our envelope offers Baby Boomers many possibilities to positively interact with others who are different from us.

Consider the values of giving back and risk taking as they apply to diversity. By the year 2020, the majority of the American work force will be made up of minorities and young women. As we age, these younger generations will be financially supporting our Social Security and long-term care. We are already hearing serious concerns being raised about the long-term viability of Medicare or Social Security. Major political changes will have to be made to ensure younger generations the same benefits older Americans receive today.

If the Boomer generation started giving something back to these young people today, and if we were willing to risk stepping out of our own current comfortable racial or cultural environments to make personal connections with people different from ourselves, it will make it easier to resolve the inevitable economic and political conflicts caused by the sheer size of our generation as we age. In addition, our ability to model, as individuals, what it means to be interdependent and multicultural will help younger generations share the unique knowledge and experience they have acquired growing up and living in a diverse society with their elders.

Activities to **ReFire** your life

Living Diversity

Take a walk through a busy area of your city or nearest city on Friday or Saturday evening. Make note of every bit of evidence you see of diversity—people and the clothes they wear, different languages being spoken, varieties of restaurants and other ethnic businesses, advertisements, and so forth.

Younger Generations *Are* the Diversity Experts

Boomers often speak with political correctness and moral certitude about the value of diversity. We have encouraged our children and other younger people to go to the same schools and play together, work together, and even live in the same neighborhoods. But our personal lives and history have often been very different. Almost all of us grew up in racially separated environments. Most of us did not go to integrated schools, play on racially and ethnically diverse playgrounds, live in integrated neighborhoods, or have many personal friends from racial or culturally diverse backgrounds. We have articulated diversity as a value, but we haven't had much of the daily, lived experience of diversity that most younger Americans experience today.

The real experts at diversity in America are the younger generations. They have had more personal experience living in a diverse culture, day to day, than any of the older generations alive today.

It is true that many of us have worked on a wide range of issues and concerns with people from diverse racial and cultural backgrounds—often at work, in the military, or at some level of political or community life. But there is a significant difference between participating in a meeting or working on a project with people of color and daily personal contact with someone different from yourself. Today's younger generations live, eat, and sleep diversity "24-7," twenty four hours a day, seven days a week!

> *"Today's younger generations live, eat, and sleep diversity '24-7'..."*

Living Diversity Intergenerationally

Engage in an intergenerational family discussion about each person's experience in working and living in a diverse culture. What have been each generation's experiences in this regard? Provide opportunities to share stories and to ask questions of one another.

Diversity Is an Intergenerational Issue

A ReFirement perspective offers us the possibility for a reverse educational process—the young teaching the older generations. For example, I had the privilege of working with an incredible group of teenagers (ages thirteen to eighteen) in Myrtle Beach, South Carolina. Half of these teens were white and the other half African-American. These young people organized a dialogue, with eighty racially diverse people representing the five living generations, to talk about they could do to prevent teenage violence in schools in Myrtle Beach. It was inspirational for me to work with these young people and see their dedication and commitment to each other across racial and cultural divides. I had the feeling we would work together again.

I was later invited to come to Saluda, South Carolina, to assist the community in a dialogue specifically about race and cultural diversity. The invitation was initiated by a Lutheran minister who convinced the South Carolina Health Department to fund my work. I immediately thought about this group of young teens. I told the superintendent of schools that he should invite the teenagers to come to Saluda and talk to other teens and adults in the high school. The teens would not talk about Saluda's racial issues directly but instead share their excitement about the experience of discussing important issues with all the generations in a community.

The Myrtle Beach teens came to Saluda and helped lay the foundations for the Saluda Intergenerational Dialogue held at the end of March 2000. Their courageous effort was a first in South Carolina—and perhaps the nation. This small southern rural city, suffering from both historical and personal racial difficulties, looked to young diversity experts to help everyone in Saluda understand how they might live better in their community.

The young people's message was simple:

1. We first need to find platforms where we share things in common, and being part of a generation is one of those platforms.
2. The resolution of any important issue needs to involve all the generations and as much diversity as there is in a community.

Activities to ReFire your life

Making More Diverse Friends

Make a list of the friends you have from other races and cultures. How much time do you spend with them each week in person, on the phone, or through the use of E-mail?

Moving Beyond Racism

I have found that many older people, regardless of their race or culture, discover that by the time they are in their seventies, eighties, and nineties, things like skin color and language become much less important in their relationships with others. Even though these elders were raised in the midst of some of the worst racist and segregated situations, many of them are not bitter.

I met an African American woman who was eight-seven, partially handicapped, and living in a racially mixed residence in the Southwest. She had grown up in Texas and lived most of her adult life working as a nurse in the South. She told stories about having to walk to rural all-black schools while white kids rode the bus. She received only textbooks that were handed down from the all-white schools, and some of them contained racist expressions that couldn't be erased. Perhaps most embarrassing for her to admit was having to bow and curtsy on the way to school if they passed a house where the white folks were outside on the porch.

Yet this same women worked later in life as a volunteer tutor in a literacy program reading to young white, African American, and Latino children. Now, she told me, some of the white women and men in her residence are really the only real family she has. She has not forgotten the racism she experienced, but she has been able forgive the people from her past and develop loving relationships with others in her new community.

When you reach seventy or eighty, there seem to be more important things to consider in close relationships than past injustices or even horrible personal treatment. As we age, we need to focus more on our commonalties as members of the human race and begin to practice the act of forgiveness.

Boomers are also in a unique position to act as intermediaries. We can lift up the lived experiences of the young, and share stories of the old who have discovered that differences seem much less important after one reaches elderhood. Through increased intergenerational dialogue, we can explore new and creative ways to understand and experience diversity in our everyday lives.

Activities to ReFire your life

Diversity Comes in Many Forms

Eat at ethnic restaurants and shop at businesses owned and operated by people of a different race or cultural heritage from your own.

Read newspapers, watch television news or movies from other countries, or listen to international public radio news to secure another perspective on issues in the world.

Read novels depicting life in other countries.

Living in the Global Village

Modern communications and technology has made the world a "global village." John Kadiec suggests that we imagine shrinking the earth's population to a village of precisely 100 people with all the existing human ratios remaining the same. Such a village would include:

57 Asians
21 Europeans
14 from the Western Hemisphere
8 Africans

Of these 100 villagers:

- 52 would be female; 48 would be male

- 70 would be non-white; 30 white

- 70 would be non-Christian; 30 would be Christian

- 89 would be heterosexual; 11 homosexual

- 59 percent of the entire world's wealth would be in the hands of only 6 people, and all 6 would be citizens of the U.S.

- 80 would live in substandard housing

- 70 would be unable to read mail

- 50 would suffer from malnutrition

- 1 would be near death; 1 would be near birth

- 1 would have a college education

- 1 would own a computer.

Kadiec adds "When one considers our world from such a compressed perspective, the need for both acceptance and understanding becomes glaringly apparent." Embracing and learning to live effectively in a diverse culture is not simply a matter of good will in our changing world. It is at the heart of our personal sanity and survival.

Recovering from Vietnam

Diversity and healing can be about much more than dealing with race, culture, or age. It can also focus on the deep wounds and divisions caused by important historical events. Perhaps the landmark division experienced by our generation was the Vietnam War. It touched almost all of us. Whole families were torn apart by differences in viewpoints, values, and the choices many of us felt we needed to make.

These deep divides still exist within some families and still separate Boomers from one another. Younger adults often tell me their parents, particularly those who served in Vietnam, still don't like to talk about the war. Consequently, the children and grandchildren of Boomers really don't know much about it. In some families today, the silence is deafening. "Nam" or "the war" still remains a conversational taboo.

In 1982, I wrote and produced the first documentary film about Agent Orange and its effects on Vietnam veterans. *Agent Orange: A Story Of Dignity and Doubt,* was the first *independent* film about chemical defoliation in Southeast Asia from the veteran's point of view. Martin Sheen contributed his voice and support for this film, giving it national and international exposure. I had the opportunity to travel around the country with the film, showing it to thousands of Vietnam vets and their families. There were many long discussions about the deep emotional pain many men and women suffered as a result of this war. Most of the veterans I met didn't know I was arrested twice for protesting the war in the early 1970s and led a major anti-war demonstration in New Mexico in 1971.

My cousin, who is four months younger than I, went to Vietnam as a combat helicopter pilot and was shot down twice. For years, he and I didn't speak to each other because of our differences over the war. After I made my film, I sent him a copy with a letter explaining that I never protested against soldiers who went to Vietnam; I was only opposing our government, which got us involved in the first place. After my cousin saw the film, we were finally able to reconcile.

If families are to mend—and if we are to heal our own lives and relationships with each other—the personal divisions caused from the Vietnam experience must be acknowledged so forgiveness and

"We need to find ways to share our stories and listen to each other's pain without judgment."

healing may begin. We need to find ways to share our stories and listen to each other's pain without judgment. For so long, the issues associated with the war (in part: who served and who didn't, and why; a deep cynicism and lack of trust in our government and other institutions; the ghosts of 55,000 young men and women with their names on a marble wall; the mental and physical injuries suffered on the battleground; and the care our soldiers received when they returned to this country) have torn at this nation's deepest values and pained many hearts. The war's aftermath left our country enveloped in grief, suspicion, guilt, and anger. It is time to close this painful chapter of our history and reconcile our diverse positions—without requiring uniformity or denial of our personal values and stories. This is a significant ReFirement challenge.

Activities to ReFire your life

Understanding Vietnam

Ask someone between the ages of fifteen and twenty what they know about the war in Vietnam; then ask someone from each of the following age groups the same question: twenty-one to thirty-five; fifty-five to sixty-seven; and sixty-eight and older. Compare their recollections with your own.

If your family has divisions that stem from the Vietnam War, talk to family members individually and ask them if there is anything you can do to heal any remaining divisions they still might experience with other family members about the Vietnam War.

There are many others divisions in America that also need attention. We have a growing gap between rich and poor. People with mental illness or physical handicaps remain the targets of discrimination. A young gay man was brutalized and hung up on a barbed wire fence and left to die.

I am not suggesting that we just beat ourselves over the head and feel guilty about what hasn't been done. Guilt rarely inspires action. Almost everyone agrees we have made significant progress on many of the issues that divide us over the past fifty years. However as our generation increasingly dominates the political and economic stage of this society, we have an even greater responsibility to use our ReFirement values and move the country in dramatic new directions.

First, let's dust off some of our old idealism and recreate the image of our generation with the benefit of thirty years of hindsight. In spite of how Boomers have been portrayed in the media—as self-centered, concerned only about their own welfare—millions of us still have strong idealistic impulses. Many of us work in low-paying careers like teaching and in nonprofits because we consider the work to be the most meaningful. Millions of us still want to make a difference.

I don't think that anyone can deny that it is much easier to be more creative and intuitive when we are feeling positive and hopeful about the world. This is the spirit we need to reclaim in the face of increasing apathy and cynicism about our major institutions and those who run them. Our children and younger generations will be excited by the emergence of the new ReFiring Boomers.

Activities to ReFire your life

Use The Web To Explore Diversity

At least two times each week, initiate a conversation with a person of a different race, cultural background, or political or religious viewpoint. Try to regularly engage in conversation with people of different ages. Seek out their perspectives. Use your computer to establish a number of E-mail relationships or join in chat rooms with different people across the world.

Language Is a Door to Diversity

Enroll in a conversational or reading course in a foreign language.

Join or create a conversation group where you can practice your new language.

The Dream of the New Millennium

On New Year's Eve 1999, we acknowledged the closing minutes of the old millennium and the entrance into the new one. Millions across this country and throughout the world paused to watch the televised arrival of the new millennium as it was celebrated, hour by hour, across the earth. For those few hours we watched people celebrate in their own traditions in the famous cities of the world, in small villages and rural communities, and in more primitive cultures. They celebrated amid floodlights and around campfires. The images and sounds of that night provided millions of television viewers with a profound experience of unity with all people on this planet. Accepting diversity and healing the wounds of divisiveness is a process that begins with our deepest dreams for ourselves and the human family. It is time to ReFire those dreams.

Chapter 8

Becoming an Elder-In-Training

As far back as history has been recorded, human beings have set aside a special role in their tribe or clan for the people with the greatest accumulated wisdom and experience. Many of the world's sacred religious texts identify an *elder* as the man or woman with the longest and most mature faith tradition. In our own country, for more than 250 years, African-Americans have referred to the oldest and wisest people of their race as "elders."

Barry Barkan, who works with older people at the Live Oak Living Center in El Sobrante, California, defines an elder as:

> . . . a person who is still growing, still a learner, still with potential and whose life continues to have within it promise for and connection to the future. An elder is still in pursuit of happiness, joy and pleasure and her or his birthright to these remains intact. Moreover, an elder is a person who deserves respect and honor and whose work is to synthesize wisdom from long life experience and formulate this into a legacy for future generations.

While on a speaking tour in northern Florida, I had the opportunity to attend a workshop sponsored by the first community-based "Age-ing to Sage-ing" program in the United States. Inspired by a book of the same title by the visionary Zalman Schachter-Shalomi, this new program was designed to help older people "be spiritually radiant, physically vital, and socially responsible." The group states that "the elders of the tribe convert rich experience into wisdom and consciously transform the downward arc of aging into an upward arc of expanded consciousness."

The Age-ing to Sage-ing folks believe sage-ing doesn't come naturally with age; it takes work to become an elder. This organization has developed a rich and dynamic process to help people assess their eldering strengths and weaknesses, to become more intentional about their elderhood.

As part of the "Age-ing to Sage-ing" workshop, I participated in a fascinating and transforming exercise. We were asked to relax in our chairs, close our eyes, and visualize sitting in an imaginary quiet room near a large staircase that was located to our right. "Go over to the staircase," the leaders instructed us, "and begin walking upward." They counted the stairs as we walked: "One, two, three, four . . ." until we reached "twelve."

At the top of the stairs was a large door that we were asked to open slowly. When we had opened the door, the next thing we would see would be the inner elder that we all have. The workshop guides instructed us to look directly at the face of our inner elder and ask that elder what was the most important thing we needed to do to make us a good elder in our older years. "Watch the inner elder's face and listen to the message you receive," the guides said.

After the inner elder delivered the message to us, we were to thank him or her, and quietly close the door, turn around, and slowly walk back down the stairs into the quiet room. Finally, we were asked to open our eyes and share what we had viewed and what our inner elders had told us.

I was amazed at what I experienced. Initially, I saw myself at my current age. Then suddenly my appearance started morphing into an older and older man who had long gray hair, a beard, and very wrinkled skin. My future self, smiling and happy, looked at the younger me and said, "The most important thing you need to learn about being an elder is to really listen to others, be compassionate, and stay involved." My inner elder smiled a yogi-like smile before I closed the door.

Rabbi Zalman says when he feels confused about life, he seeks an audience with the inner elder. "I enter his marvelous chamber and bask in his wisdom and love. When I share my confusion with him and ask for suggestions, they come less as action directives than as perspectives. When I see clearly what lies before me and what is required of me, my confusion lifts and I move on to the next stage of my journey."

I found my journey to a future self to be deeply mean-ingful because it gave me a new perspective on my experi-ence of growing old. For a few minutes, I was really present with my older self and happy with the voice I was hearing.

Activities to ReFire your life

Meet Your "Inner Elder"

Try repeating the "inner elder" exercise. What did your elder look like, and what did he or she say to you?

As Boomers, we are not yet old enough to be considered elders, nor do we have sufficient life experience to offer "wisdom." But we can see ourselves as "Elders-in-Training."

The "Elders-in-Training" label also fits well for a generation that has raised the level of training to an art form. Every major corporation, government agency, and educational institution promotes its unique, specialized training programs. Although thousands of job and hobby trainings are now available, few educational opportunities address how we might grow older with wisdom.

In ReFirement we will first learn how to treat our own elders with respect, caring, and compassion. Through this, Baby Boomers can demonstrate to young people how we would like to be treated in our older years.

Secondly, we can begin to show young people that we are also ready to begin a lifelong commitment of service to them. Right now, many opportunities exist for Boomers to mentor, work in literacy programs, coach sports, volunteer in schools, and become Big Brothers or Big Sisters.

A special note on becoming an elder and on lifelong learning: Many of us moved from our poor and working-class roots because of education. I remember some radical friends in the early 1970s not understanding the pride I had in my Ph.D. I told them I had worked very hard driving a cab, getting scholarships, and doing odd jobs to be able to get that degree.

One way we can all give back to younger people is to commit ourselves to being always curious and expanding our own learning. Then we can share our passion for learning with those younger and older than ourselves who need role models to show them how important learning and education are in our society.

Intergenerate Your Life

Propose that your neighborhood, municipality, faith community, or school celebrate Intergenerational Week during the third week of May. Work with others to develop creative ways for recognizing the gifts and talents that each generation brings to community life. (Refer to Resources section in Chapter 11 and Fred Ramstedt for further information on celebrating Intergenerational Week.)

Look through a daily newspaper or a weekly magazine such as *Time* or *Newsweek.* Cut out a sampling of miscellaneous articles, quotations, and advertisements. Review all the material you clip, and divide it into two piles: One pile should represent what you think is useless information and the other pile what you believe to be genuinely important information. Ask a younger or older person, or even a Boomer friend, to share their opinions with you. Try to be nonjudgmental about the choices and comments they make.

Ask yourself this question: "What is the most significant thing I am doing in my life right now that is having a positive impact on another person?" Write down your response and reaffirm or revise it every six months.

Boomers As "Real" Elders

At some point, Boomers will move from being Elders-in-Training to become the actual elders of the early twenty-first century. All younger generations will be looking to us for leadership because of our education, spiritual vitality, and our other ReFirement values.

We will have many serious issues to confront. Here are four that I believe will dominate our "elder watch."

1. The environment
2. The widening gap between rich and poor
3. Participation in our democracy
4. The danger of increased personal isolation and separation

1. **The Environment: A Response by "Environmental Elders"**

   The Boomer version of environmental education in grade school during the 1950s and 1960s, was coloring in Smokey the Bear comic books. Today, young children are talking to astronauts thousands of miles above the earth and witnessing the ever-widening hole in the ozone layer from outer space. Through the Internet, children across the globe talk with each other about the number of species that human beings help render extinct each year and the steady destruction of the rain forests. They share conversations about the polluting of the great oceans that, in turn, leads to killing or poisoning great mammals, fish, and other aquatic forms of life.

   Today, children also discuss the millions of new man-made chemicals that affect every part of the environment. They can recite data on global warming and air pollution and its effect on rain and snowfall patterns worldwide. They cry out to adults to listen, but many adults seem much more preoccupied with profits and consumption than they are with conservation and stewardship.

It's not true that Boomers and elders from older generations don't care about the environment. Some of us went back to the land in the 1960s and 1970s, practicing self-sufficiency and appropriate technology. We are largely responsible for the steadily increasing popularity of the organic food movement and the financial support of groups like the Sierra Club, the Land Trust, and Nature Conservancy. We have built a recycling and environmental clean-up industry in this county that didn't exist twenty-five years ago. And many of us who go camping, hiking, hunting, and fishing love the earth and believe in maintaining a sustainable environment.

In spite of all we have done, young people are telling us that we are not doing enough. Many of them believe we are in a major crisis. They say the environment for Boomers is just any other issue like taxes, Social Security, or abortion. But for the two younger generations in America, the environment and how we treat it, is *the* foundational issue. It takes precedence over all other issues. Younger people in large numbers believe that without a healthy and functioning ecosystem, every

> "For the two younger generations in America, the environment and how we treat it, is the foundational issue."

other issue will become quite irrelevant. Younger generations are pushing us to make a *primary* commitment to the environment. Pure water and clean air, a balanced ecosystem in which all species and plant life are respected, living and thriving oceans, stewardship, and conservation—will be among the most important issues confronting environmental elders in this century.

As Elders-in-Training, Boomers can help the young create a much broader based environmental movement by sharing our organizational and media skills. We can help transform older established environmental organizations into more intergenerational organizations with all generations represented in leadership roles. As Elders-in-Training, we can walk our talk about the ultimate perils of conspicuous consumption on the planet by living simpler lives. It is so important to model how to integrate an environmental ethic and consciousness into our everyday lives. Finally, everyone—young and old—can ask themselves how current political and economic practices and policies will affect the most vulnerable of all: the generations yet unborn who cannot speak for themselves. Only as we begin such actions, will we be respected as authentic "environmental elders."

> *"As Elders-in-Training, we can walk our talk about the ultimate perils of conspicuous consumption on the planet by living simpler lives."*

Know Your Environment

Seek opportunities for involvement in environmental issues. For example, gather a group of people of different ages to participate in an environmental clean-up activity. During the activity, ask the young people what they are really concerned about and how you might be of help. Consider giving the important young people in your life good books, compact disks, or videos that explore the care of the earth and environmental issues. Be creative about where you get the materials. Check out library book sales, rummage and garage sales. Encourage the youth to pass the materials to another person. Recycle the knowledge!

2. **The Widening Gap Between Rich and Poor: The Response by "Compassionate Elders"**

   In spite of the expanding United States economy, low inflation rates, and poll after poll reporting consumer confidence, a large elephant that few people in government or industry want to see still sits in our societal living room. In the United States and the world, there is a growing gap between the wealthy and the poor. The highest percentage of the homeless in the U.S. are families with young children. The largest number of people living in poverty are single women and children. Millions of Americans cannot afford even the most basic preventive medicine. It is ironic that all of this occurs in a booming economy. Ralph Nader points out that Bill Gates has a greater net worth than the bottom 120 million working Americans make in salary and benefits each year.

If these numbers continue to grow, the disparity between rich and poor will negatively affect the quality of life for all of us. The more affluent individuals will want to protect their material assets by isolating themselves in gated and secure communities. The have-nots will be left to fend for themselves, because many social service safety nets have already disappeared. Such economic disparities will exacerbate racial tensions, because many of the poor are people of color.

As a result, we could be at risk for the development of a more authoritarian system of government. The wealthy could use their considerable power and influence to protect themselves by passing more restrictive laws and giving increased powers to police to protect private property. These new protective initiatives would be aimed at the growing number of have-nots who believe they have nothing to lose by breaking laws and social mores.

This dreary scenario is based on what could happen in a growing and dynamic economy. Imagine what would happen if we had a sudden major economic downturn? What if our current economic boom were to turn into an economic bust? In this case, the gap between rich and poor could become a major crisis for the entire society. Millions of people would be looking for someone to blame. Centuries old, but unresolved, racial and ethnic fears and wounds would almost certainly deepen. In such a scenario, compassionate Boomer elders would be prepared to offer wise and balanced leadership.

Today, compassionate Boomer Elders-in-Training can lead the way in finding creative ways to include as many people as possible in the American Dream. During this time of "prosperity" (for many—but not for all) Re-Firing Boomers can support public and private investment in better education, good housing, access to quality preventive medical care, more individual entrepreneurism, and the guarantee of a decent standard of living for all of our citizens. Wise elders of a nation should do no less.

3. Participation in Our Democracy: The Response by "Citizen Elders"

It is alarming that fewer than half of the registered voters in this country elected the last two presidents in the twentieth century. What is even more disturbing is that the decline in voting is seen every age group. Millions of Americans, including myself, feel we no longer have a real voice in our democracy. We believe special interests own the political system and use it for their own bidding. This is a dangerous trend, one partially caused by the Baby Boom generation itself.

Young Boomers learned early that organized groups such as large corporations and labor unions had a much greater influence than individual citizens when petitioning their government. We saw people in large interest groups exercise control of the political agenda. Today, thousands of new "special-interest groups" largely started by Boomers, promote their own narrow agendas. When these single issue or interest agendas are coupled with billions of dollars of influence money being pumped into the political system, we are at great risk of creating a volatile "anti-democracy" mixture.

As citizen participation dwindles, special-interest groups acquire a disproportionate amount of power and influence in both national and local politics. We are seeing a dangerous downward cycle: as fewer citizens participate, more favors are given to those who can afford to buy them—leading to more public cynicism and even less public participation.

People ask me what I think the most important issue is in any political campaign. I tell them the most significant issue in any campaign is how many people are actually going to show up and vote.

As citizen Elders-in-Training, Boomers could exert a great deal of influence by making citizen participation the number-one political issue in an election cycle. Boomers need to support the most radical and far-reaching proposals for campaign finance reform. We can also lead the way in searching for political solutions to problems like health care and entitlements, by looking for solutions that serve the common good rather than the

"As citizen Elders-in-Training, Boomers could exert a great deal of influence by making citizen participation the number-one political issue in an election cycle."

narrow agendas of the special interests. Such actions will, I believe, be respected by both younger and older citizens and provide Boomers with more credibility as we become responsible "citizen elders."

4. **The Twin Dangers of Personal Isolation and Separation: The Response by "Connecting Elders"**
We are in the middle of a major economic, political, cultural, and social transformation. At midlife, Baby Boomers are witnessing and actively participating in the dawn of a new age driven by technology and a highly interdependent global-information network.

We may forget that the general public began to use the internet only in 1993. While it is impossible to predict what the new information-based society will look like in another ten or twenty years, we are undeniably rushing headlong into a new and very different future—and we are doing so on fiber optic cables at the speed of light!

As connecting Elders-in-Training, we can continually remind the new high priests of the information age that rapidly increasing the development and speed of technology can have serious and profound effects on human development.

In his book *High Tech/High Touch: Technology and Our Search for Meaning,* John Naisbitt says we have become intoxicated by technology. We fear and worship it. Because it is so dominant in our lives, we tend to blur the distinction between what's real and fake. Naisbitt says the antidote is high touch—the impulse to embrace the real, the natural, the authentic, the wholesome. This is exactly what ReFirement offers to Boomers.

I once heard a lecturer speculate about the sudden disappearance of the Mayan civilization. The Mayans built an incredible empire based on their abundant production of corn. As they became wealthier and their society became more complex, they began to rely more and more on their high priests for expertise and direction. Over hundreds of years, the experts developed more complex rituals for deciding when to plant crops and when to harvest. Farmers literally forgot when the growing seasons began or ended. According to the lecturer, when Mayan farmers exchanged their personal connection to the land and natural cycles for a reliance on experts who got lost in abstractions and complexity, the once mighty Mayan empire essentially disappeared.

The lesson of this story for Connecting Elders is not to allow the new information high priests and fiber-optic prophets to forget the basic need humans have for face-to-face interaction. As we get deluged with billions of bits of information every day, it will take many wise Connecting Elders with experience, vision, and values to help prioritize what information will be most helpful in building a "web" of healthy human connections. It will also take these wise Connecting Elders to help us see what information isolates and separates us from one another.

Activities to **ReFire** your life

Listen and Learn

When conversing with a younger or older acquaintance, concentrate on your role as listener and learner. Paraphrase some of the things they say so that you are sure you understand them to demonstrate to others and confirm for yourself that you are really listening. Take some notes if you find this to be an easier way to remember what people are saying.

To practice listening and learning from someone younger or older than you, sit in on a chat-room discussion on the Internet. There are thousands of chat rooms, designated by age, in which you can be a quiet observer. If you want, you can also ask a question or engage in the conversation. Represent yourself and your age by being honest about who you are. If you ask a question, try clarifying questions first. Let people know you are really interested in finding out information and you are not there to judge their opinions. Later, you can take what you have learned on-line and engage in personal face-to-face discussions with people of other generations.

ReFired, Elders-in-Training will learn how to transmit positive values and experiences from one generation to another, be encouraging and empowering of others, open to surprises, ready to share compassion and a helping hand to people in need. These elders will also pay close attention to the spiritual dimension of their lives. They will need to answer the question of what truly spirits them?

Activities to **ReFire** your life

Become a Servant Leader

Contact your local volunteer center, religious congregation, or a neighborhood agency and inquire how you might explore opportunities for service, such as: mentoring or tutoring children or teens, assisting older people, or working on any of the issues discussed in this chapter.

Qualities of a Good Elder

How do you rate on the following characteristics? Give yourself a rating based on a 1–5 scale where 1 point represents those that you believe need much more development on your part and 5 points represents those attitudes and behaviors that you think you strongly exhibit.

	I Need More Development			I Strongly Exhibit	
Being:					
loving	1	2	3	4	5
nonjudgmental	1	2	3	4	5
tolerant	1	2	3	4	5
open to surprises	1	2	3	4	5
encouraging	1	2	3	4	5
empowering	1	2	3	4	5
appreciative	1	2	3	4	5
sensitive to the feeling of others	1	2	3	4	5
patient	1	2	3	4	5
listening	1	2	3	4	5
interested in other people's stories	1	2	3	4	5

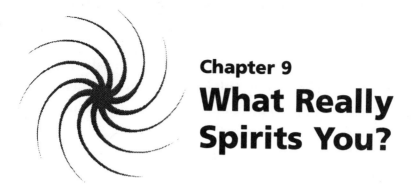

Chapter 9
What Really Spirits You?

The actress Jane Fonda inspires many kinds of feelings and reactions depending on your political perspective. At the age of sixty-two, she said she finally "recognized her own power and acknowledged faith in a higher one." She likens her life to a movie script made up of three acts. "As an actress I know how important the third act is. You can have first and second acts that are interesting, but you don't know what they mean. Then a good third act pulls it all together."

The psychiatrist Carl G. Jung also wrote about the role of religion, spirituality, and meaning in the last third of our lives. His writings speak of an inner voice that at some point in our later life calls to everyone across race, culture, or nationality and says, "What is my life all about?" The way we go about answering the "meaning" question can result in a tremendous new source of personal energy and spirit.

The search for our spirit or spirituality is lifelong, a journey that takes many turns. We may start out looking for new energy to achieve our goals and then discover those goals are not really what we thought they were. We reorient ourselves toward newer and truer aims.

Most people associate spirituality with organized religion. Millions of Americans find that institutional religion—as experienced in churches, temples, or mosques—provides opportunities for deepening their spirituality, expressing their faith through worship, and finding a place to belong in a supportive faith community. Others have been wounded by the churches they grew up in or have never found a spiritual home and are still seeking.

We do well to remember that spirituality predates all organized religions; spirituality has been a part of the human life since people first achieved a sense of consciousness. The theologian Cletus Wesels tells us that spirituality "has permeated the evolution of the human race for over three million years." His colleague, Diarmuid O'Murchu, says "spirituality is written into the weaving and unweaving tapestry of evolution and creation. Creation itself is the source and wellspring of spirituality."

This chapter will focus on the root of spirituality, namely the *spirit*. In the original Hebrew, the word *spirit* literally means alive, breath, and engaged. Regardless of our faith tradition or other belief systems, a good dose of spirit in our lives will contribute toward making us stronger and better ReFirees.

> *"Regardless of our faith tradition or other belief systems, a good dose of spirit in our lives will contribute toward making us stronger and better ReFirees."*

The Search for Spirit

A good question for each of us to ask ourselves is "What spirits me?" Some other words that help us understand the characteristics of spirit are "passion," "energy," and "aliveness." Can you remember situations and experiences that left you feeling energized? Times when you felt energy surge from the top of your head to your toes? What are the occasions when you feel really alive? What activities engage your passions?

On the other hand, remember situations that have dulled you. This dullness could have included a sense of mental and physical fatigue, as if you are just going through the motions of living without having a clear sense of meaning or purpose. It is a flat, joyless feeling.

Look at the culture we live in. During almost every waking minute of our lives we are bombarded with messages about materialism and consumerism. Think about how many times a day you have been asked to buy something because it will help make your life better. Then think back on all the things you have bought in your life and how many of them have truly made you feel alive, energized, and passionate for an extended period of time.

At this point in our lives, we Boomers have had our share of temporary ups and downs. All of us have experienced loss and pain. But what I am talking about in this search for our spirit is a prolonged sense of either feeling alive or feeling dulled and bored with life.

As we approach and pass midlife, we often discover that we feel burned out. We begin to wonder if our life amounts to much. This is the time when many of us discover that, though we have many material goods, our material accumulations throughout the years do not leave us with any sense of inner abundance. We may have worked hard at jobs we merely tolerated or even despised in order to acquire more of what society says is the "good life." We find, however, that such a life does not feel good to us any more. We ask ourselves, "Is this all there is?"

Jean Morris Trumbauer, an author and international authority on spirituality, suggests we might reflect on these basic questions: "In what directions are the large and small decisions of my life leading me—toward greater self-esteem, aliveness, wholeness, health, love, and justice? Or toward isolation and alienation, fear, prejudice, resignation, and a gradual death of self?" The responses to these questions mark an important difference between being spirited and being dulled.

So, what spirits you? Being in nature? Exercising? Prayer or meditation? Reading a good book? Relaxing while you sit on your porch or patio? Celebrating with friends? Going to work in the morning? Spending time with your spouse, children, and close friends? Engaging in interesting conversations with other generations? Being involved in activities that demonstrate compassion and bring greater justice to our society? Living with integrity and authenticity?

What dulls you? Being constantly bombarded with information and commercials throughout the week? Working eighty hours a week? Being stuck in a job you really don't enjoy? Avoiding exercise and eating unhealthy food? Spending too much time alone or too little? Letting others run your life?

Identifying What Spirits You

Identify your experiences of being spirited and being dulled by filling in the following chart.

I am spirited by . . .	I am dulled by . . .

After you have completed your columns, take time to write a little more about a few situations (perhaps two to three) that enliven your spirit and a few that make you feel dull. If you can, talk about these with a family member, close friend, or colleague.

Start building more time into your schedule for the experiences that spirit you. Start backing off of the activities that dull you. Form an intergenerational support or discussion group in which each participant will commit to small steps in a new course of spirited life and support others in their efforts.

After you develop your list of what spirits you, make a commitment to engage in one of those activities this week. Afterward, reflect on your thoughts and feelings during that experience. Plan another activity from your list from the following week.

Review your list of what dulls your life. Replace a couple of those activities with ones from your spirited list and write them in your calendar for this month.

Taking Time for Reflection

Rediscovering our sense of being spirited includes taking time for personal reflection about what brings meaning and purpose to our lives, about what allows us to express our unique talents, styles, gifts, and passions. It also involves seeking a better balanced life—a balance among activities of self-care, quiet time, relationships, work, and citizen involvement. We may need to slow down from the busyness of life in order to reenergize ourselves. This makes it easier to engage in a personal course correction and go down new paths that inspire us and assure us our life can be full of meaning, so that we can make a real contribution to the larger society.

One of my spiritual advisors is a Lutheran minister who regularly takes personal sabbaticals to find renewal and direction in his life. He gets away from his familiar surroundings and spends time doing manual labor, eating healthfully, reading, listening to music, visiting friends, and writing. After his sabbatical, he comes back to his job, facing what we all would face if we took off for a couple of weeks or months: mountains of phone calls to be returned, work and mail piled up on his desk, and decisions that need to be made. But my friend would tell you that the time he spends to find his spirit is worth every second it takes for him to get caught up.

Personal reflection, seeking the sources of our feelings of being spirited, and leading a more balanced life will also help us respond to change in creative ways rather than experiencing personal and societal change as a constant source of stress.

Becoming a spirited ReFiree is a challenging process. Because of the diversity of the Boomer generation and its particular values, Boomers will start on the path of spirituality at many entry points:

- Ron starts each day with two strong cups of coffee, his journal, and a spiritual book he is reading.

- Maria discovered her spirit is energized by singing, so she joined a community choir.

- Phil, a busy vice-president of multinational communications corporation finds his energy in silent retreats at a Carmelite monastery, even though he is not Catholic.

- Sue is a loyal Episcopalian who has found her spirit and new energy by attending classes in Buddhist Mindfulness Meditation and practicing daily.

For some, it may take reading some books or listening to audiotapes or CDs in the car, just to understand what options they have to begin their new spiritual journey. Others may want to search on the Internet to see the diversity of spiritual web sites which await them. Others may want to search out spiritual guides to help lead them on the search for becoming more alive and spirited.

Bringing Spirituality Down to Earth

Designate a small portion of your garden or flower bed (even a flower pot) as your spirit garden. Write each of your discoveries regarding your sources of energy, passion, and dreams on an ice cream stick and plant them in the soil or sow real seeds. Each planting represents a personal dream or passion that you want to plant in this next stage of your life. Remember to water and weed your spirit garden regularly.

Make a list of the kinds of activities you engage in that cause you to lose track of time. You might ask someone close to you to tell you when they notice that your voice picks up speed and sounds enthusiastic. What are the topics of conversation that bring this response from you? These occasions and topics may help you clarify your deep passions in life. (Adapted from *Created and Called*, p. 135).

A Spirited ReFirement Story

Unlike most women in her generation, Emily was college educated, had a professional career, and was a single mother who raised three children while she worked. Her early career was primarily in social work, and she ended up working with a state agency on aging. Her job was to make sure local area agencies were doing what they said they would do. She often felt stifled and frustrated, but had three children to support and was not far away from retirement—with a comfortable pension.

While working, she started her first ReFirement by going back to school and taking noncredit courses in biology and outdoor recreation. Emily loved biking and the outdoors, but she struggled over how to turn these passions into making a living for her and her children.

After quitting her government job, she finally landed the job of her dreams. She became the Outdoors Recreation Manager for a large county park system. This was her passion and for twelve years she put her entire body and soul into it. But even though she loved her job, she found that she was not really able to balance her personal life and work. Her life became one big blur. At the age of fifty-six, Emily burned herself out on the very goals she had worked so hard to accomplish. She realized she had to get her life back in balance. What had once really "spirited her" now seemed to dulling her spirit.

Emily got a one year, nonpaid sabbatical and during this year she lived out another dream. She bicycled across New Zealand, England, Ireland, and Wales. During those long hours on the road, she had time to think and reflect about her life and once again find her spirit. She realized her next calling was to help other people, young and old, live out their dreams, regardless of their circumstances. Emily now had a new passion.

She started her own motivational speaking and workshop business called Make It Happen Inc. She scaled down to a simple lifestyle. Her mission was now more important than her monetary balance sheet.

When her friends were less than enthusiastic about Emily's new direction and perhaps a bit envious of her new energy and spirit, Emily realized that many people will try to talk you out of making your dreams happen because of their own fear. "They try and put their own fear on you," she says, "but don't listen to them. You shouldn't base your life decisions on the basis of what other people think they can't do!"

Today, Emily is the mentor for a young woman on welfare. She also teaches literacy for adults. And she is extremely happy with her life direction. "My work keeps me alive. I tell people of all ages, when you can describe your dream, then plan, focus, take risks, and be determined. You will never regret it!'" Emily is testimony to the fact that we can be "spirited" many times in our lives. The question is, "Will we be ready and able to catch the spirit when it arrives?"

> *"Will we be ready and able to catch the spirit when it arrives?"*

Consider Finding a Spiritual Life Editor

Many Boomers would find the assistance of a personal guide like Emily very useful. I am proposing that we create Spiritual Life Editors who will help us incorporate ReFirement principles and values into our daily lives. They will help us edit out our dulling attitudes and behaviors to support our goal of being spirited.

As a producer, writer, and director, I have worked with many film productions. My first experience with a film editor and mentor was life altering. I brought the vision for a film, the raw footage, and the script to this editor. With his guidance we took many hours to review rolls and rolls of film footage and log every frame. When the overall review was completed, my editor began to ask basic questions, such as, "What are the simplest and most compelling audio and visuals for this film?" "Which sounds and pictures will best tell the story?" I painfully grimaced as more and more of my sounds and images were left on the cutting-room floor. Some of these images had taken a great deal of time to capture and seemed very important at the time they were recorded. But in the final editing process, I found some of the most mundane things I had recorded and filmed took on a new significance. They told the core of my story with a simple elegance that I had not anticipated before the editing process. This is one of the wonderful surprise gifts that come from good editing.

Spiritual Life Editors could fulfill much the same role for us as that film editor did for me: namely to help us identify the core sounds and pictures of our own stories. As Boomers passing midlife and now approaching the elder years, it is essential that we capture and update the central spirited storyline of our own lives. Author James Conlon writes that "through story we discover meaning and the experience of being truly alive."

Although we are the authors of our own life stories, these stories can evolve with the guidance and wisdom of a Spiritual Life Editor. They can listen, ask questions, offer support, help us delve more deeply into our lives, and give us important feedback. They also can suggest options that we might explore and let us know when the plot line of our lives has become unfocused or even dull.

The selection of a Spiritual Life Editor can be one of the most important choices you make as a ReFiree. Choose someone other than your spouse, children, or other close family members. You might want to consider a pastor, as I have done, or a priest or rabbi. You could also ask someone whose spiritual life journey you respect and admire. Spiritual Life Editors should be able to share some of their own life journeys, be authentic and honest, not too dogmatic or controlling, and unafraid to provide direct feedback and warm support. Look for people who have enjoyed and learned from their own experiences and who continue to search out exciting visions for their futures.

"The selection of a Spiritual Life Editor can be one of the most important choices you make as a ReFiree."

At some point you may find that part of your own legacy will include having served as a ReFirement Spiritual Life Editor for someone else.

Activities to **ReFire** your life

Finding a Spiritual Life Editor

Write down several characteristics you would like in a Spiritual Life Editor. Then make a list of people who might serve in this capacity for you. This person may be a colleague or friend. You could trade your Spiritual Life Editor services with those of a friend. Or you may prefer to seek a paid professional who is trained in this or similar work. Ask acquaintances for recommendations.

Take your time. You can interview several potential Spiritual Life Editors. Tell them about your hopes and expectations. Inquire about their styles, gifts, preparation for this role, and their familiarity with the principles and values of ReFirement.

When you think you have found the right person, meet for a couple sessions. Then, together, you can discuss whether the two of you are a good match and if so, continue with a more long-term commitment to working together.

The Quest for Meaning

This chapter would not be complete without mention of one of my most significant spiritual inspirations: Viktor Frankl and his book *Man's Search for Meaning,* based on his experience living in a Nazi death camp. I read this book as a freshman in college in 1963. During my life it is the only book I have read more than ten times—cover to cover. Every time I read it, it gives me renewed energy. If Frankl was able to get through the horrific experiences he faced and still find the spirit to live and grow stronger as a human being, I certainly can meet the small life challenges I face with more confidence and hope.

Although there is so much in the book that helps me understand what it means to be alive and more spirited in my life, here are four Frankl lessons worth sharing:

1. We are radically free to make life choices. If we don't make these choices, they will be made for us.
2. It does not really matter so much what we expect from our lives but what life expects from us.
3. When life poses important questions to us, our answer to these questions must be made from a place of responsibility.
4. To paraphrase the old Nietzsche quote, a person who can find meaning and inspiration can bear almost any outward situation.

For me, the most poignant moment in Frankl's book is when he is forced to take off all of his clothes, have all of his body hair removed, and stand naked before his Nazi captors. He is separated from anything and anyone familiar to him. He has lost complete freedom over his life and death. And yet, Frankl is able to find meaning in his utter nakedness and survive one of the most deplorable situations a human being can confront. Frankl's experience is one of unbounded courage, hope and spirit.

We need spirit to cope with the major crises that are a natural part of everyone's life: the loss of a job, the break-up of a relationship, a serious accident or illness, the loss of a loved one. But we also need spirit to deal with the "daily-ness" of life—the small demands, the everyday duties—and to find some meaning and joy in them. Spirit energy can help you too as you review what you have learned so far and as you start to develop your Individual ReFirement Plan.

Activities to ReFire your life

A Spiritual Assets Inventory

Create an inventory of the most important spiritual assets you currently have to offer someone else?

Chapter 10

Developing Your Individual ReFirement Plan

You now understand the basic principles of ReFirement and the promise it offers to Boomers and people of any age. By working through some of the ReFirement exercises you have begun to see what these exciting ideas mean to you personally. Now it is time to pull together your thinking into your Individualized ReFirement Plan.

In a traditional retirement paradigm, planning for our elder years has been almost exclusively around issues of financial resources and housing. An Individual ReFirement Plan, however, is about a great deal more than the ups and downs of the market and the size of our 401k plans. To lead a meaningful and satisfying life past age sixty, you will want to balance your financial concerns with reflection and planning about the nonfinancial aspects of your ReFirement years. ReFirement calls for assessing *who you are* and *what you want to do* with the next several decades of your life.

Boomers in Their Elder Years

How does one get beyond today's marketing hype that says we *need* hundreds of thousands or even millions of dollars to retire in a comfortable lifestyle? Perhaps, we first need to reexamine our basic assumptions of how Boomers will enter their elder years.

One of the assumptions millions of Boomers seem to believe is that we need to accumulate stuff endlessly. Those that have the most toys win! But what do they win? George Carlin, the comedian many of us grew up with, had a classic routine about how people needed more stuff just to store the stuff they already had!

However, many Boomers are now joining the vanguard of a growing "simplify your life" movement. Groups like the New Road Map Foundation are "dedicated to lowering consumption in North America while increasing the quality of life." Their national best-selling book *Your Money or Your Life,* by Joe Dominguez and Vicki Robin has influenced millions toward a new frugality that honors quality of life without blind consumerism.

Our children and grandchildren are seriously questioning whether five percent of the world's population should be consuming more than sixty percent of the world's resources. If we change our focus from accumulating stuff to simplifying our lives, we will probably need less money in our later years—or at least have the extra money to direct in more altruistic directions.

If the ReFirement movement is successful, we can assume that quality health care and long-term care will be provided for anyone who needs it. Every aging American in financial need will receive free or low-cost prescription drugs. Catastrophic long-term-care insurance will ensure

that people will not lose their homes and treasured possessions if a major illness strikes, requiring personal nursing or
home care. We will take more personal responsibility for our
health care by emphasizing wellness and prevention.
Boomers will be more open to the application of both mainstream and alternative forms of medicine. If these resources
were in place, what would one really need for a meaningful
life after age sixty-five?

Of course, financial planning is important, and there are
many excellent resources to assist Boomers. Most people in
the Boomer generation probably deserve to hear that they
have procrastinated in preparing for their financial futures.
But, however old you are, it is never too late to begin seeking
appropriate financial advice.

Besides interpreting the glut of financial planning information and marketing materials that are sure to increase in
your snail mail or E-mail, you may want to question what
your focus should be for the next ten
or fifteen years. Savvy ReFirement
pioneers know it is unwise to count
on a single activity or one life direction to provide us with a consistently
satisfactory level of future returns. In
order to ReFire successfully, it is
important to have a diversified
personal life portfolio as well as a
financial one.

> *"In order to ReFire successfully, it is important to have a diversified personal life portfolio as well as a financial one."*

We can develop strategies that invest our talents and
energy in a number of meaningful personal commitments,
knowing that any one of them might turn sour or, in the final
analysis, not yield us the satisfaction we had anticipated. We
can also pull all our personal and generational assets

together to build the most effective ReFirement portfolio possible. Our most valued investment will be our most personal one—our values, our talents, our health, and our energy—ourselves!

Starting Your
Individual ReFirement Plan

So, how does one begin assessing personal capital as well as financial capital? Here are some simple steps and exercises to get you started on the ReFirement planning process. If possible, set aside a few hours on an evening or weekend when you won't be disturbed.

If you have ever worked with a financial or life planner, imagine that person is in the room with you now. We are going to start by looking at your personal assets and liabilities. What do you think they are and what do others close to you think they are? Among your assets you should include: skills, personality traits, values, important relationships, networks, and finances. Liabilities might include physical or psychological weaknesses, negative life experiences, deficiencies in education or training, or bad habits.

Because we can't always see ourselves well, choose at least one other person you trust to help you identify your assets and liabilities. Be sure to choose someone who is kind as well as honest. If you don't feel comfortable asking someone, use your imagination. Picture yourself talking with a compassionate parent, your favorite sibling, or a supportive friend. Ask her or him to help you name your strengths and your liabilities.

Using your ReFirement journal, copy the following chart and begin to fill it out:

Example:

	My Assets	My Liabilities
My View	Personality Traits Experiences Possessions Contacts	Personal handicap Workaholic Perfectionist
Others' View		

Be sure to "mine your assets" in order to get the most complete list possible. For example, in a workshop I did on ReFirement a woman said she "made dolls," seemingly ashamed to name dollmaking. I asked her to list all the skills she needed to have to make a doll. That list included: reading a pattern, creating clothing, drawing, sewing, knitting, measuring, and patience. After she was able to "mine her assets," she felt much better about filling out her asset list. Also feel free to add additional assets, anything you feel are resources that help you to live well for the next thirty years. Add items that come to you in the next week or two.

Now it is important to see the things you listed as liabilities turn into potential assets. This is much easier to do if you complete the following exercise:

Example:

My Liabilities or Weaknesses	How They Might Be Seen as Assets
I have a physical handicap.	I can be more sympathetic or empathize with others who have handicaps.

Now that you have honestly looked at both your assets and liabilities, it is time to examine how you might use your assets in ReFirement. This exercise includes a comparison between how you have used an asset in the first half of your life and and how you might want to use it differently in the second half. I've given some examples to jog your thinking.

This exercise will help you translate your past skills into new projects in the future. When you finish this part of the planning, you will be able to break away from the constrictions you often place on yourself or those that others place on you. This exercise will also help you plan for how to use your skills in new and fresh ways in ReFirement.

Example:

Asset	First half of my life	Second half of my life
Organizational skills	Helped me succeed in my corporate job	Help a non-profit get on track
Intelligence		
Compassion		
Sense of Responsibility		

Now it is time to seriously look at how we currently are spending one of our most precious commodities—our time—and how we would like to spend that time in our ReFirement years. How often do you hear people tell you, "I just don't have the time"? The reality is you make time for those things you determine are most important.

Here is a fun exercise to look at your present and future "energy use." First, list approximately how much time you currently spend doing what you do. Then list how much time you would like to spend on each exercise in ReFirement. Don't worry about getting it exactly right. The point is to see the big picture. This exercise will give you a good snapshot look at how you spend your time.

Example:

How much time do you/will you currently spend in a day on. . .	Now	In ReFirement
Work	8 hours	4 hours
Self-improvement	1 hour	6 hours
Leisure	2 hours	4 hours
Maintenance		
Sleep		
Eating		
"Giving back" (e.g. volunteer time)		
[insert as many items as you want]		

Now let's look at how you spend your money. Using the same chart, get out your checkbook and your credit card receipts for the past three months and write down what you are spending money on now and what you would like to spend in your ReFirement.

With any of these exercises, you can begin to bring your expenditures of time and energy in line with your self-chosen values. ReFirement begins when you want it to.

Now it is important to connect your assets and your values into possible actions or activities by creating a "personal mission statement" and setting some long term goals. Before you do this, you might want to review the values you identified at the end of Chapter 1.

A Personal Mission Statement and Long-term Goals

In midlife many of us become more acutely aware of the preciousness of our time and energy. According to studies, our perception of time changes as we age. Time goes by faster. A new sense of urgency sets in. We realize we are no longer able to postpone doing what we have felt called to do but have put off for "some day" in the future. In midlife, the future becomes *now*.

"In midlife, the future becomes now."

At age forty-five, I sat down and created a simple mission statement for the next twenty years. It reads: "I will devote the next twenty years of my life promoting intergenerational respect, caring, and coopera-tion." Although my specific ways of doing this work have changed over time, the major outlines of my commitment remain the same. My overarching mission is *broad* enough to incorporate many different kinds of goals and activities. But it is also *specific* enough to provide guidance for accepting or turning down paid and nonpaid opportunities that come my way. My commitment provides clear boundaries for much of my everyday decision-making; thus it serves as a helpful stress reducer.

Almost every business and not-for-profit I have worked with realizes at some point that they need a mission or vision statement. This statement includes the ideals they want to accomplish over the long haul. The best statements I've seen are short—no more than a paragraph or two—and to the point.

Take some time and compose a mission statement for the next twenty years of your life. What would you like to see yourself accomplishing? Don't worry about the "hows." What's important is your long-term outlook. You might want to begin, as I did: "I will devote the next twenty years of my life. . ." Don't worry about getting the mission statement perfect. You can always refine it—or even change it altogether.

Example:

MISSION STATEMENT

I will devote the next twenty years of my life promoting intergenerational respect, caring, and cooperation.

Every year I sit down on December 31, and ask myself, "What have I done this year to fulfill my mission? What do I want to do next year to add to my mission accomplishments?" I will review my mission and accomplishments at age sixty-five and see if I want to continue it, make changes or develop a completely new mission.

It was an important revelation to me to realize that I would not accomplish my entire mission within my lifetime. As you begin to implement your own life plan for your middle and elder years, you will likely reach a similar conclusion. Our work and our lives are not ours alone. They are always in service to future generations.

> *"Our work and our lives are not ours alone. They are always in service to future generations."*

Another ReFirement Pioneer Story

Fortunately there are many people I call "ReFirement Pioneers" who are models for aging Boomers trying to create their ReFirement plans. Richard Morgan is a friend of mine from Morganton, North Carolina. Richard was a college professor, a parish minister, and the father of three Baby Boomers. After his retirement, he experienced what many retirees experience after successful careers are put to bed. As Richard says, "I went from 'who's who' in my community to 'who's he'?"

Richard came from a long line of distinguished Protestant clergy who worked on prestigious campuses such as the Universities of Pennsylvania and Kentucky. He followed in his father's footsteps and taught and counseled at Wake Forest University. Eager to get away from academia, Richard became a pastor for a small rural church in North Carolina for the last ten years of his formal professional life. During all of his teaching and pastoral ministry, Richard always had a desire to write and publish, but he was either too busy or didn't have a focus for his writing. At last, he thought he was ready for retirement and a new writing career. He had done careful financial planning and believed he was prepared for this new stage in his life. But he was in for a big surprise.

Richard says the first year of his retirement was very difficult. He experienced depression and later developed a serious illness requiring surgery, leaving him physical incapacitated for the first time in his life. He began to wonder if he would always be this physically limited.

During his recovery time, he began thinking about how little time is spent working with the nonfinancial issues regarding retirement—specifically, the spiritual and emotional issues that older people face. This realization gave Richard a new focus and life purpose. He helped pioneer and popularize the field of spirituality and aging.

After writing six books and giving hundreds of presentations, he has this advice for ReFiring Boomers:

- Expand your horizons and do things unlike anything you have every done before. You need to find meaning for your later years. The brilliant psychiatrist Erik H. Erikson wrote, "The last stage of life is either spent in integrity or despair. You will not despair if you believe your life has meaning."

- It is important not to go along with what the media and the dominant culture is telling you. You need to decide for yourself what your mission and life values are. Be rebellious!

- Try to find a creative balance between remaining active and finding time for your inner life. Being too busy can be a form of violence against yourself. It is essential for busy Boomers to start taking time now for the life of their souls and their spiritual growth.

- Be a responsible elder by mentoring someone younger than you. This is how to stay connected to both the present and the future.

Richard Morgan is ReFiring every day, and he says he will continue to do so as long as God gives him the gift of years and experience.

Pulling It All Together

Now is a good time to take your financial planning information and combine it with your ReFirement data. Your new Individual ReFirement Plan should be more holistic, value-based, passion filled, and driven by a continuing search for meaning in your life. Because you have taken the time to look deeper and more authentically at yourself and the future, there is no danger that someday you will wake up and realize you have been living somebody else's vision of your third age.

> *"Your new Individual ReFirement Plan should be more holistic, value-based, passion filled, and driven by a continuing search for meaning in your life."*

The final part of the ReFirement planning process is to consider your legacy: How do you want to be remembered?

Chapter 11

Claiming Your Legacy

My greatest fear about growing older was that I might become *insignificant*. As time passes and my vision of ReFirement becomes clearer, I feel much more hopeful this will not happen. I believe that becoming a part of the ReFirement movement will also make you feel more confident about your future.

As you reflect on how to feel more confident in yourself and have an impact on society, consider the story of my ninety-five-year-old friend Fred Ramstead. He lives with his wife of sixty-two years, Louise, in an intergenerational apartment complex in San Francisco, where they are the oldest and longest living residents. Both Fred and Louise have trouble getting around and need assistance for getting anywhere. Fred also suffers from painful arthritis in his hands but does have two index fingers that still work. Fred does not take any pain medication, because, he says, "The pain reminds me I'm alive."

At eight-six, he read a story in the San Francisco *Examiner* by a nine-year-old boy about how he caught a fish. Fred says, "The young boy had a gargantuan imagination. The imagination and talent exhibited by this boy captured my heart." He sat down and wrote the boy a letter telling him how much he loved the fish story. In doing so, Fred realized that the joy he felt in connecting to someone from another generation should be shared by every adult in our society. Fred thought that a week should be set aside as "Intergenerational Week"—a time for all generations to share the gifts and joys each brings to the others. As Fred says, this week would become America's most inclusive celebration because "everyone is a member of a generation." Then, hunting and pecking with his two usable index fingers, he started typing letters on his old manual typewriter, and sent them to the Rose Bowl Parade organizers, U.S. political leaders, major world figures, and many service groups. He urged people to set aside the third week of May each year to celebrate the gifts and talents of all generations. Because of Fred's diligence and hard work, Intergenerational Week is now officially celebrated in two Canadian provinces, in many communities across America, and is becoming better known in Europe and Asia. Fred recently received a Lifetime Achievement Award from the national organization, Generations United, in Washington, D.C., for his tireless efforts to promote Intergenerational Week. He says, "It is never too late to do something you passionately believe in."

No matter what our age or physical condition, the spiritual, intellectual, and emotional parts of our lives will also always be changing. We will navigate these shifts more gracefully if we adopt an attitude of acceptance toward both the short- and long-term life transitions that we encounter. This is where ReFirement comes in. I am confident that if you follow the ReFirement principles and activities outlined in this book—and approach them in a spirit of playfulness— you will age, like my friends Fred and Louise, with maturity, dignity, and purpose.

Creating Your Ethical Will

Assuming you are able to successfully ReFire, what would you like to leave as a legacy? Now is the time for each Boomer to start to think about his or her legacy and take the necessary actions to create it. Your legacy planning can begin by creating an "ethical will." We have all heard about "living wills," (that put you in charge of dying with dignity) and regular wills, (that distribute your material possessions) but ethical wills are much less well known.

The idea of the ethical will comes from Jewish tradition. Jews believe that, in addition to passing down possessions from generation to generation, we also leave the next generation our values and beliefs. Rabbi Jack Riemer of Miami has written a wonderful book on ethical wills titled, *So That Your Values Live On.* He says an ethical will ". . . is a document which explains what the writer has learned about life. It offers the next generation the wisdom the writer has achieved." Another person who is experienced in developing ethical wills is Barry Baines, the developer of the Ethical Will Web site, www.ethicalwill.com

Either Rabbi Riemer or Barry Baines can assist you in learning how to write an ethical will. One of the most useful things about such a document is its changing nature over time. As you go through your ReFirement, you can add to or subtract from your ethical will. I recommend reviewing and revising it once a year—perhaps make it a New Year's routine. (Firefighters recommend replacing smoke detector batteries on New Year's. Why not "recharge" your ReFirement "batteries" at the same time?) This practice will be a great way to review the past year and begin a new one.

You might want to consider adding your ethical will as an addendum to your regular will, ensuring it will be read after your death. Or you might want to ask your family and closest friends to an annual reading and discussion of your ethical will.

Each ethical will is unique, but here are some themes usually included:

- a list of important personal and spiritual values
- hopes for future generations
- blessings for future generations
- lessons of one's life
- statements of forgiveness and requests for the forgiveness of others.

An ethical will is not a legal document but an outline of what the writer really believes and why.

> *An ethical will is not a legal document but an outline of what the writer really believes and why.*

Given these basic parameters, here is an example of the **2000 A.D. version of the Ethical Will of James V. Gambone.** I hope you will use it as an aid in writing your own.

My Personal Values

After fifty-one years of living in the United States and about three years spent between Colombia, Mexico, China, Japan, Costa Rica, the Dominican Republic, England, Sweden, and Canada, I have developed some basic personal values that I hope make me a good person who contributes to the world. As I see it, these values are:

- listening to what others have to say
- expressing compassion for those who have had fewer opportunities than I
- being honest in personal and business dealings
- keeping my word
- speaking out against injustice toward people, animals, or the environment
- recognizing that I am not perfect and not expecting perfection from others
- giving a full effort to all I am doing and expecting the same kind of effort from those who work with me
- respecting differences—knowing not everyone thinks, acts, or believes as I do
- being kind and friendly to strangers
- having the courage to be countercultural

- being a loving and caring husband, godfather, and dog dad
- believing cooperation is a better value than competition
- walking my talk—trying to model what I talk about in my work
- being known as person of integrity

My Hopes for Future Generations

I hope:

- we find a way to have peace with social and economic justice in every nation of the world
- all human beings are able to develop whatever talents they have within them
- we treat animals and all living things with the same respect we have for our own species
- we treat the environment as a delicate ecosystem which enables all species to enjoy life
- hatred is replaced with love
- people of earth can get beyond the concept of the nation state
- all generations will show respect, caring, and cooperation for each other through personal contacts and relationships in the new information age
- all religions and expressions of faith see each other as complementary and not competitive

- spiritual values become more important than material ones
- no person on this planet dies from hunger, insufficient housing, or lack of care
- the true measure of our humanity becomes how well we treat those who are not able to take care of themselves
- every day is a new adventure in which we can help each other become better human beings

My Blessing for Future Generations

I wish that all generations might claim the blessings of: compassion, hope, love, reason, honesty, integrity, balance, belonging, risk taking, a lively inner child, faith in something beyond the material, good spirit, longevity, a high quality of life, solitude, health, good luck, well-being, charity, and humor.

Life's Lessons

Here are ten life lessons I have learned so far:

1. I need to take care of myself and my family. If I am not able to do that, it is very difficult for me to take care of others.
2. I cannot change another human being. No matter how hard I try, people will change only if they decide to change themselves.
3. Positive reinforcements always work better than negative ones.

4. Never assume anything.
5. Not all issues are equally important to me. No person is capable of righting every wrong committed in the world. I must pick my causes carefully.
6. Love will ultimately win out over hate.
7. I live my life on the premise that most people are basically good.
8. It is important to have as many varied experiences as I can, otherwise I will make decisions based on very limited personal knowledge.
9. Don't take things for granted—especially the people you love.
10. There is something beyond this life. That is what gives real meaning to my rather temporary—and sometimes painful existence—as a human being.

Every year, I plan to add more life lessons to my list.

Forgiving Others and Asking for Forgiveness

I want to forgive everyone who has done any harm to me in my life and ask for forgiveness from anyone I may have harmed. *[Go ahead and list people here if that helps you to commit to forgiving. To protect yourself and the privacy of other people, you may want to keep parts of your ethical will confidential.]*

As I ReFire, my ethical will will grow and develop. The wonderful thing about ReFirement is that the process can begin at any age. Baby Boomers are the principal target of this book but people in their twenties or even their eighties can ReFire whenever they choose and create their own ethical wills. It's a good tool for people of all ages to help them understand who they are.

I invite you to think about your legacy and use the ethical will as the starting point for your own personal legacy statement. I am eager to hear from you and learn from your personal ReFirement stories and experiences. You can contact me through ReFirement.org.

A ReFirement movement will enable the Boomer generation to use our size and experiences to create more opportunities for exploring our human potential. I believe that, as a generation, we have been given an abundance of gifts—both personal and generational. By identifying and using these gifts to better ourselves, our society, and our world, we can continue to make a real difference.

"This ReFirement movement will enable the Boomer generation to use our size and experiences to create more opportunities for exploring our human potential."

I am convinced this is our generational destiny. And to carry our our destiny, we need to network with others and build a larger ReFirement movement.

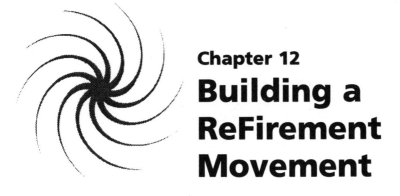

Chapter 12

Building a ReFirement Movement

Personal changes are hard to make. The force of habit and the conforming pressures of the culture are strong. It might take six weeks or more to incorporate a new habit or life change.

In making any kind of change, it helps to have group support. That's why people join AA, a weight-watching group, or an exercise club. As Boomers we also have a strong need to belong. These needs for belonging and support can be met in at least three ways:

1. **By forming a ReFirement group**
2. **Asking your employer to have ReFirement parties when people "retire" from their jobs**
3. **By helping to create a virtual worldwide ReFirement web movement**

Forming a ReFirement Group

You can form a ReFirement group in your community of faith, neighborhood, workplace, or community organization. It doesn't have to be a big group. You might start with one partner or with two or three people. You probably don't want the group to be bigger than ten so everyone feels comfortable and has a chance to share.

Begin using this book as a guide. Have each person commit to reading a chapter before your meetings and doing the ReFirement exercises at home. When you come together, give each person time to say which ideas were most helpful or interesting and to share as much of their answers to the ReFirement exercises as they wish.

An alternative: Gather as a group and take turns reading a chapter out loud. Then take time individually to answer the ReFirement exercises for that chapter. One person at a time could share what they have discovered.

This book could also be the basis for a weekend retreat, alternating activities to take place in solitude, with group sharing sessions.

Throw a ReFirement Party at Work

I have been approached by a number of human resource professionals interested in exploring how to have a ReFirement party replace the typical retirement party. Believe me, people in the workforce are more than ready to get rid of the black balloons, the horribly ageist greeting cards, and the typical speeches, "thanking you for valuable service to this organization." For all the time we have spent on the job, we deserve something far more creative and meaningful.

I am developing a number of specific ReFirement party programs for businesses, nonprofits, government, and faith communities as a follow-up to this book. These parties will all be based on the following five principles:

1. Instead of just celebrating years of service, we need to celebrate the assets of the ReFiree and let everyone know how these assets made everyone's life more meaningful at work. Encourage people to tell stories about how a particular quality of the ReFiree helped them personally or on the job.

2. Any kind of greeting cards given the person leaving work should be positive and supportive of ReFirement goals and objectives. (This will probably mean making them yourself until ReFirement captures the attention of the major greeting card manufacturers.)

3. ReFirement parties should be intergenerational, including younger and older friends of the ReFiree from outside the workplace.

4. In any formal presentations at the party, it should be made clear the person is not just *leaving from*, but really *going to* a remarkable new stage in their lives. You might want to consider giving them a beautiful flame in the form of crystal or gold. This will reinforce and concretely symbolize the regenerative and reenergizing symbol of fire.

5. Ask every person who speaks at the gathering to end by giving a personal blessing to the Refiree.

You can get the ball rolling at your office when the next person comes up for retirement. Ask if they would be interested in having a ReFirement party instead!

Have a ReFirement Party!

Plan your own ReFirement party. What would you like to see happen? Who would be there? Where would it take place?

Help Create a ReFirement Web

The United States is at the edge of a major historical, economic, and cultural transformation—the beginning of what we are calling the "information age" and the graying of seventy-six million Baby Boomers. Some social commentators are comparing the effects of the new service-based, information economy to the dramatic societal changes at the onset of the Industrial Revolution.

"The United States is at the edge of a major historical, economic, and cultural transformation. . ."

I invite you to think about contemporary communications. Some years ago, I produced an audio and video teleconference that took place between Minneapolis and London. After the signal left our studio in Minneapolis, it was transmitted by microwave to a transponder twenty-five miles away. The transponder relayed the signal to a satellite high above the equator. This satellite transmitted the signal to a relay transponder in Maine, which in turn sent it up to a satellite serving northern Europe. The satellite sent the signal to a microwave receiver located on the Tower of London, which sent the signal to a studio in downtown London. This entire process took place in less than half a second!

Today, computers and E-mail are becoming as common as the telephone. But, there is a digital divide. Many people, mostly poor and people of color, do not have personal access to the Internet. Yet huge capital investments in fiber optics, broadband communications, and multimedia compression technology almost assure that within a short time, anyone with a television or a telephone will have easy personal access to some part of the Internet and the World Wide Web.

Today, we can instantaneously connect with each other, share information, send materials in all forms of media, sign petitions, contribute money to causes we believe in, join organizations, and buy products and services. We can do almost anything over the Internet that our imaginations allow.

Here are some interesting facts to consider about the history and potential of the internet and the web:

1. The internet and the world wide web began on a very small scale in 1993.
2. The world wide web doubles in size almost every five months.
3. As of March 5, 2000, there were nearly 16,000,000 web sites registered worldwide.
4. The largest survey ever done of internet users in the United States finds that nearly half of internet users are women. People over sixty-five are a rapidly growing sector. Eighty-three percent of internet users are registered voters!

I find the last fact most interesting and relevant to promoting ReFirement principles and actions. Overall, the participation on the web is growing by leaps and bounds in every age group while, at the same time, participation by voters in our democracy is declining in every age group. In 1996, the president of the United States was elected by less than half of all the people eligible to vote. Elections are no longer determined by the people who vote; they are determined by the people who stay at home.

The internet and the world wide web will soon offer every citizen in this country a direct voice in every major sector of American life. It is hard to find a company, government agency, or a politician without a web site. Any new voice can present information on the web without having it filtered by media, business, religious, or political censors. A large ReFirement movement can begin and grow on the world wide web.

"We can use the internet to accomplish the first major goal of ReFirement: retiring retirement."

We can use the Internet to accomplish the first major goal of ReFirement: retiring retirement. If only a few million of us dedicated ourselves to ending this debilitating and unnecessary system within our lifetime, we could begin a virtual nationwide dialogue on how to make it happen. The web and the internet offer us the least expensive and most inclusive ways to reach people quickly and coordinate a national agenda for action.

I believe ReFirement principles can be a catalyst for using information technology to create the broadest based virtual movement ever seen in the United States. Boomers who believe in ReFirement will ultimately need their own web site, and/or the use of existing web sites, to grow and nurture their virtual movement.

In this rapidly changing world of information technology, it is premature to say exactly how all of this will develop. But the following are some basic principles that can provide the foundations for constructing the ReFirement web site:

- The site can provide a simple mission statement about ReFirement: What it means and how we are hoping to grow a grassroots, ReFirement movement among the seventy-six to eighty-four million Baby Boomers and anyone else who believes in ReFirement principles.

- The site can always be in development. ReFiring Boomers, and others who support the ReFirement concept, will be able to decide what topics they think the site should develop and suggest ways to keep the site alive and growing.

- If any commercial product or service is offered on the site, it can always be offered as one option among the best comparable products and services available. The site might offer the ReFirement "seal of approval" based on objective and well-researched information about any commercial offering.

- The site can be very interactive.

- The site can be fun, upbeat, a little edgy, and really focused on ReFirement. It is this focus which will give us our unique place on the information superhighway.

- No one who registers on the site will have their names sold to "spammers."

- The site can have links to the best quality, content-specific sites on topics such as financial planning, health, intergenerational connections, books, tapes, and so forth. These sites, in turn could agree to promote ReFirement goals and concepts.

- The site can be audio, video, and data capable.
- The site can be easy to use and designed to serve both high- and low-tech users.
- The site can reflect the diversity of the Boomer generation: women and men, people of color, those with disabilities, those with differing sexual orientations, and so forth. This can be achieved in part by having sections of the site inviting diverse, personal ReFirement stories, organizing chat rooms, and by connecting Boomers to already existing web sites dealing with a wide range of Boomer interests and opportunities.

When ReFirement enters the information super highway, it will rapidly gain momentum because it directly and honestly addresses the needs of an aging country in a period of rapid revolutionary change. ReFirement provides a comprehensive vision that includes acceptance of our own aging, choices for intergenerational relationships, a balanced approach to living, and idealism about the future. Moreover, ReFirement provides millions of individual Boomers with practical suggestions for how to develop personal action plans. As Elders-in-Training, Boomers can use the new technology to learn more about our environment and ecosystem, narrowing the gap between rich and poor, exciting all generations to participate in a political system, and ensuring that as many people as possible feel a personal sense of connectedness and belonging as the dizzying whirl of change speeds by us every day.

ReFirement on the Web

Imagine you could design a ReFirement web site. What would you want from this site and how would you like to use such a web site? What web sites have you already visited that you'd like to see linked to www.ReFirement.org? What information would you start seeking from it immediately? How might it help you get started on ReFirement?

When you have in mind the major dimensions you'd like to see in a ReFirement web site, imagine a conversation with your Boomer friends and colleagues. What would you tell your friends to encourage them to visit the site for the first time? What might their questions be?

One Person Acting with Courage Can Still Make a Difference

I know many of my friends who are suffering from "compassion fatigue." They are caring people who want to make a difference in the world. They look at the forces and powers that seem to control the media, the government, and business, and they believe it is impossible to really change the system.

I like to remind them about the story of Rosa Parks. Rosa is a small, frail, elegant woman in her eighties. As a young person, she had the courage to risk her life in Montgomery, Alabama, by refusing to go to the back of the bus.

In the South at that time, anyone who stood up for civil rights risked their own life and/or the lives of their family and friends. The legal system and the armed police who enforced it were both on the side of segregation. When churches were bombed and young innocent children were murdered, it was easy to become discouraged. But in spite of what seemed like insurmountable obstacles, Rosa and thousands of other courageous freedom fighters did not give up. Murders, arrests, bombings, police brutality, and other forms of physical and emotional violence did not deter their struggle. They persevered and built a civil rights movement that gave them the personal support they needed to continue pressing for change. the important point here is that before it became the large civil rights movement, it was individuals like Rosa and others who made *personal* decisions and then acted to fight for freedom.

The images of Rosa Parks being arrested and nonviolent men, women and children attacked by police dogs and fire hoses were seen nightly by millions of young Boomers in their living rooms. Television and the electronic media were major factors in moving public opinion to support civil rights and in educating an entire generation of young Americans about the need for correcting more than three hundred years of injustice.

Just as the new media of television in the 1960s helped end legal oppression for millions of Americans by building a mass consciousness around the need for equal opportunity and justice, the internet and new information technology can help transform the way we look at the entrenched institutions and legal systems we have built around the current retirement system and aging in general.

The ideas embodied in ReFirement come at a perfect time in American history. Everyone is becoming aware of the impact seventy-six million aging Boomers are having, and will continue to have, on our society. A mass consciousness is beginning to form around the issues of how our generation might spend our elder years. We can expect every presidential election for the next eight to twelve years to include aging Boomers trying to define the character, destiny, and legacy of their generation. A ReFirement movement will help us speed up this process of definition. It will also aid us in our search for personal fulfillment and meaningful community, while allowing us to exert a significant influence on the revolutionary political, economic, and cultural change the world is going through.

We can work together to end retirement as we know it. We can accept our own aging, promote the values of belonging, giving back and risk taking, share our Elder-in-Training stories, stay meaningfully connected with all generations, simplify and balance our lives. In doing so, we will regain a sense of optimism and adventure about the future. ReFirement is about hope and opportunity. It is about creating a new movement. As Robert Kennedy said, "Few will have the greatness to bend history itself, but each of us can work to change a small number of events, and in the total of these acts will be written the history of this generation." Millions of Boomers, joined by their allies in older and younger generations, can and will dramatically change our society and culture for the better. Through the small and not-so-small actions of each of us, we have the greatness to enrich the legacy of our generation and generations to follow.

"ReFirement is about hope and opportunity."

Activities to ReFire your life

Building a ReFirement Movement

Find a ReFirement partner or study group.

Contact the web site and share your comments about the book and what you are thinking about for your ReFirement.

Think about the hardest goal you have ever accomplished and then make a list of the personal qualities it took for you to accomplish that goal. Share that list with the ReFirement web site.

Think back on the movements you have read about or participated in (e.g., the labor, civil rights, peace, women's, or environmental movements.) What lessons have we learned from these movements that can be applied to ReFirement?

Resources
Further reading, people, and Web sites

Chapter 1: Boomers—Who Are We Really?

Further Reading

Gambone, James V. *Together for Tomorrow: Building Community Through Intergenerational Dialogue*. Crystal Bay, Minnesota: Elder Eye Press, 1998 (phone 800-586-9054, www.pointsofviewinc.com or contact Amazon.com)

> This book contains the rationale for why a generational perspective is important in looking at community, business, or faith issues. It also introduces the Intergenerational Dialogue™ process which brings the generations together under the banner of respect, caring, and cooperation.

Strauss, William and Neil Howe. *Generations: The History of America's Future 1584 to 2069*. New York: William Morrow, 1991.

> An in-depth and provocative look at American history from a generational perspective. The authors believe that four generational types recur throughout American history. According to the authors. if you subtract eighty-eight years from your birth date, you will find a generation similar to your own. They also suggest that if generations repeat themselves in history it is possible to predict the future by simply looking at our present generations.

People

Barbara Jensen has written a number of articles about working class culture and values. She is an adjunct faculty member at Metro State University in the Twin Cities, Minnesota, and is also in private practice as a psychologist. She is writing a book called the *Silent Psychology: The Inner Lives Of the Working Class.* She is available for keynote speeches, presentations, training, and workshops on issues related to social class for a variety of audiences, including: healing professionals, clergy, educators, and corporate human resource professionals. Barbara can be reached at 612-822-9172 or at bjensen@tc.umn.edu

Chapter 2: Turning Aging Upside Down

Further Reading

Friedan, Betty. *The Fountain of Age.* New York: Simon & Schuster, 1993.

> Ms. Friedan is thorough in discussing how men and women age and about the social impact of aging in the U.S. She presents a vast amount of research data coupled with the stories of real people (including herself) on their aging journey. This is a hopeful and helpful book.

Gambone, James V. *All Are Welcome: A Primer on Intentional Intergenerational Ministry and Dialogue.* Crystal Bay, Minnesota: Elder Eye Press, 1998 (phone 800-586-9054, www.pointsofviewinc.com, or contact Amazon.com)

> This book is written specifically for faith communities. It shows that these communities are the only voluntary communities left in America in which all generations gather at least one day of the week to do

something beyond their own self interest and if every
faith community in America was an authentic intergenerational community of faith, our society would
be dramatically changed for the better.

Saussy, Carroll. *The Art of Growing Old: A Guide to Faithful
Aging.* Minneapolis: Augsburg Books, 1998.
   A friendly, informed guide about growing as we age,
   releasing new possibilities for creativity, spirituality,
   and fulfillment. Includes suggestions for activities,
   questions for reflection, and guidelines for group
   discussion.

People
If you would like to get in touch with a Foster Grandparent's
program like the one mentioned in this chapter, you can find
them in your phone book under "Foster Grandparents" or
call your local area agency on aging and ask them for information on a Foster Grandparent's program in your area.

Web sites
For the most comprehensive intergenerational links on the
World Wide Web, go to the Resources & Links page at
www.pointsofviewinc.com.

Chapter 3: Let's Retire Retirement!

Further Reading
Sinetar, Marsha. *Do What You Love, the Money Will Follow:
Discovering Your Right Livelihood.* New York: Dell Publishing,
1987.
   An organizational psychologist helps us find our right
   work, no matter what our age.

Chapter 4: Getting Your Groove Back

Further Reading

Csikszentmihaly, Mihaly. *Flow: The Psychology Of Optimal Experience*. New York: Harper and Row, 1990.

>   *Flow* discusses how we can regain happiness in our lives. It presents research from a variety of disciplines to help us understand how we can have optimal experiences in our daily lives.

Frankl, Victor. *Man's Search For Meaning*. New York: Washington Square Press, reprint 1998.

>   *[Author's note:* Man's Search for Meaning *is truly a classic. I read this book as a freshman in college in a philosophy class on existentialism. Since then, I have re-read it countless times. When I teach—regardless of the course—it is required reading for my students. The students often do not understand why they are reading this book for a marketing class, or for a documentary production, until they finish it. Then they realize that every subject they study is about meaning and how we find meaning in our lives. If someone reading* ReFirement *did nothing more than discover Frankl's book, they would learn many of* ReFirement's *most important lessons.]*

Chapter 5: Taking Charge of Your Own Health

Further Reading

Siegel, Bernie S. *Love, Medicine, and Miracles*. New York: Harper & Row, 1986.

>   A medical doctor and cancer surgeon shares what he has learned about the spiritual aspects of health and healing.

Dossey, Larry. *Healing Words: The Power of Prayer and the
Practice of Medicine.* San Francisco: Harper, 1993.
 Drawing on both science and spirituality, Dossey, a
 medical doctor and expert on alternative healing
 provides new perspectives on the relationship
 between prayer and healing.

Kabat-Zinn, Jon. *Full Catastrophe Living: Using the Wisdom
of Your Body and Mind to Face Stress, Pain, and Illness.* New
York: Delta Books, 1990.
 From the program of the Stress Reduction Clinic at
 the University of Massachusetts Medical Clinic.
 Draws on yoga and mindfulness meditation.

Web sites

Here is a list of Web sites that I have found helpful while
researching this chapter on health and life balance. These
sites also have links to other useful sites. You should also
search the Web under: wellness, health, alternative medicine,
and holistic health.
 berkeleywellness.com (One of the oldest wellness
  newsletters in the U.S.)
 www.vix.com/pub/men/health/health.html (on
  men's health issues)
 www.mayohealth.org
 www.healthwatchers.com
 www.healingwell.com
 www.healthwell.com
 www.wellnessbooks.com
 www.webofcare.com
 www.ofrf.org (Organic Farming Research Foundation)

Chapter 6: Men Are from Mars. Women Are from Venus. But We Both Live on Earth!

Web sites
Women's issues:
> www.wiser.heinz.org/mainpage.html (representing
> > Women's Institute for a Secure Retirement-WISER)

Men's issues:
> www.refdesk.com/men.html
> www.vix.com/men
> www.virtualfreesites.com/reference.men.html

Chapter 7: Changing Through Healing and Forgiveness

Web sites
To secure a copy of *Agent Orange: A Story Of Dignity and Doubt,* contact www.pointsofviewinc.com

The sites I have found most helpful in researching this chapter have been:
> www.forgiving.org (represents the Campaign for
> > Forgiveness Research)
> www.forgivenessweb.com
> www.forgiver.net

Also search the Web under the word "forgiveness."

Chapter 8: Becoming an Elder-In-Training

Further Reading
Straub, Gail. *The Rhythm of Compassion: Caring for the Self, Connecting with Society.* Boston: Tuttle Publishing, 2000.

Uses personal stories and exercises for reflection to help us balance our inner and outer lives, for self-growth, and social action.

People

Paulette Geller and **Allison Isson** of the Age-ing to Sage-ing Center in Winter Park Florida are excellent resources for learning about the process developed by Rabbi Zalman Schachter-Shalomi and Ronald Miller. To contact the SAGE-ing Center in Florida, call 407-629-5771 or E-mail Allison at aisson@wphf.org

To contact **Rabbi Zalman Schachter-Shalomi** either call the Spiritual Eldering Institute in Boulder, Colorado, at 303-449-7243 or E-mail to spiritelder@aol.com

Chapter 9: What Really Spirits You?

Further Reading

Adams, Kathleen. *Journal to the Self: 22 Paths to Personal Growth.* New York: Warner Books, 1990.
> A good basic book on how to use journaling techniques for personal insights and development.

Moore, Thomas. *Care of the Soul: A Guide for Cultivating Depth and Sacredness in Everyday Life.* New York: HarperCollins, 1992.
> A psychotherapist and expert in Jungian psychology shows how you can add spirit, depth, and meaning to your life by caring for your soul.

Thompson, Peg. *Finding Your Own Spiritual Path: An Everyday Guidebook.* Center City, Minnesota: Hazelden, 1994.

A psychologist and social worker who leads spiritual exploration groups for women, helps seekers (especially those who have been turned off by organized religion) to discover a spirituality that fits their values and lifestyle.

People

Jean Trumbauer has been a tremendous inspiration and help in writing this book. She is also available as a consultant on a wide range of spirituality issues. Contact her at:

Jean Morris Trumbauer
Trumbauer Consulting
4302 Fourteenth Avenue South
Minneapolis, Minnesota 55407-3226
Phone: 612-823-7706
Fax: 612-825-2520
E-mail: trumbauer@aol.com
Web page: http://members.aol.com/trumbauer

Emily Kimball is also available as a speaker and workshop leader to get you "spirited" in a hurry! Emily has great stories to tell, and her experiences will be valuable for all ages. Emily can be reached by E-mail at etkimball@aol.com or by phone, 804-358-5536 (Eastern time).

Richard Morgan gives dynamic workshops and keynote speeches on the topic of spirituality and aging. Look for his book, *Fire In the Soul: A Prayerbook for the Later Years*, Nashville: Upper Room Books, 2000. You can contact him directly at rmorgan@hci.net

Ted Bowman is a personal friend and one of the nations leading experts on "the loss of dreams." He has worked in Northern Ireland and travels throughout the U.S. conducting workshops and speaking about healing and rediscovering your dreams. Ted can be reached by phone, 651-645-6058 (Central time) or by E-mail at bowma008@maroon.tc.umn.edu

Chapter 10: Developing Your Individual ReFirement Plan

Further Reading

Foster, Richard. *Freedom of Simplicity.* San Francisco: Harper, 1981.

A contemporary Quaker writer gives the rationale and practical ideas for living a simpler and freer life.

Kallestad, Walt. *Wake Up Your Dreams.* Grand Rapids: Zondervan, 1996.

An inspiring and practical strategy to help you discover your lifelong dreams and turn them into reality.

Leider, Richard J. and David A. Shapiro. *Repacking Your Bags: Lighten Your Load for the Rest of Your Life.* San Francisco: Berrett-Koehler Publishers, 1995.

A practical book to help those in the second half of life evaluate where they've come in their journey and how they want to move on.

Chapter 11: Claiming Your Legacy

People

Fred Ramstedt, in his nineties, still loves to get calls from people interested in Intergenerational Week. He can be reached by phone at 415-584-0053 (Pacific time).

[Author's note: Fred has passed the mantle of Intergenerational Week to me for the year 2000. If you can't get in touch with Fred, please contact me at pointsofview@earthlink.net. In 2001, Intergenerational Week will be housed permanently at Generations United, in Washington D.C. Contact Generations United at www.gu.org or 202-662-4283.]

People and Web sites

For more information on the ethical will concept or to purchase the Ethical Will Resource Kit, send an E-mail to info@ethicalwill.com or contact the Web site of Barry Baines, www.ethicalwill.com. Rabbi Riemer's book, *So That Your Values Live On* is available from Jewish Lights, P.O. Box 237, Route 4, Sunset Farms Offices, Woodstock, Vermont, 05091.

Chapter 12: Building a ReFirement Movement

Web site
www.refirement.org

 **Chapter Notes**

[Author's note: There is only one footnote in the entire book. (It is in the first chapter and refers to the census data proving that seventy-five percent of Baby Boomers came from poor, working class, or small family-owned businesses and farms.) The purpose of foot-notes, as I have understood them for three decades as a professor and adjunct faculty member, is to be sure proper credit is given for someone else's idea and to be sure a quoted passage is not taken out of context. Having guided many people through their Masters thesis and Ph.D. dissertations, I can assure you that giving a citation with a page number can only tell you if the writer misquotes the original source. It will not tell you if he or she has taken the quote out of context. You usually have to read the entire book to determine that. I have not included page numbers for that reason.

This Chapter Notes section is my way of bending traditional publishing guidelines and "reader unfriendly" style rules. My intention is to meet the requirements of proper scholarship while making this book easier to read. I give full credit to every idea that isn't my own in this Chapter Notes section. For the person who wants to see if I plagiarized or took something out of context, or for readers who want to go further intellectually, look to the Resources section for additional information.]

Introduction: Why ReFirement?
As mentioned in the text, I came across the words "ReFiring" and "ReFirement" in a short conversation I had with Dr. Roy Fairfield a few years ago. I have not talked to Roy specifically about this concept since our initial conversation. All the ReFirement ideas found in this book are my own.

The complete citations for the two books referenced in the Introduction are: Cirlot, J. E. *A Dictionary of Symbols.* Second Edition. (New York: Philosophical Libraries 1971. And Eliade, Mircea. *Myths, Dreams and Mysteries.* (London: 1960).

Chapter 1: Boomers—Who Are We Really?

This chapter is a culmination of eight years of work and research. Much of what is written here came from conversations with hundreds of Boomers I have met from across the country and in facilitating my Intergenerational Dialogue™ process. It also came from reflecting on my own experiences as a Boomer. I also referred to my own book, *Together for Tomorrow: Building Community Through Intergenerational Dialogue* while preparing this chapter (see *ReFirement*, Resources, Chapter 1).

When the opportunity came to write *ReFirement*, I went to the University of Minnesota library thinking it would be easy to find the breakdown of Boomers by class or family background. Working with the best research librarians, we were unable to find any specific data or other material that really helped me.

One afternoon, I was looking over the *Historical Statistics Of the United States,* Bicentennial Edition, published in 1975, (see figure 1 on next page) and I discovered part of my answer under a category called "Major Occupation Groups of the Experienced Civilian Labor Force, 1900-1970." If you take the 1950, 1960, and 1970 census data, you find that roughly 72% of all people holding jobs in the United States were manual and service workers, clerical workers, farm workers and managers, and small proprietors. If you add to that the unemployed or "poor," as they were officially called before 1965, the figure rises near or a little above 75%.

These blue collar, farm-related, small business owners, and heads of families with moderate or very low incomes were also the parents of 75% of all the Baby Boomers. If we use 76 million Boomers as a base, that means approximately 57 million Boomers came from these backgrounds.

I immediately called David Morgan who teaches Planning and Sociology at Portland State University. He had just edited a peer reviewed article for the scholarly journal *Generations* called "Facts and Figures About the Baby Boom." He confirmed my data by looking at the same census reports in his office. He said he was not aware of anyone else who had written about this characteristic. I knew I had discovered something important but now I had to find out more.

Figure 1 ————————————————————————————

From *Historical Statistics Of the United States,* Bicentennial Edition, published in 1975.

Major Occupation Group of the Experienced Civilian Labor Force, Both Sexes: 1940 to 1970

(In thousands of persons 14-years-old and over, except as indicated.)

Major occupation group	1970		1960		1950		1940
	16 years old & over	14 years old & over	1970 classi-fication	1960 classi-fication	1960 classi-fication	1950 classi-fication	
Total	79,802	80,603	67,990	67,990	59,230	58,999	51,742
White-collar workers	**37,857**	**36,131**	**27,028**	**27,244**	**21,253**	**21,601**	**16,082**
Professional, technical, & kindred workers	11,561	11,018	7,090	7,336	5,000	5,081	3,879
Managers, officials, & proprietors	6,463	6,224	5,708	5,489	5,096	5,155	3,770
Clerical and kindred workers	14,208	13,457	9,431	9,617	7,132	7,232	4,982
Salesworkers	5,625	5,433	4,799	4,801	4,025	4,133	3,450
Manual & service workers	**39,420**	**36,947**	**33,377**	**33,207**	**29,749**	**30,445**	**26,666**
Manual workers	29,169	27,356	25,475	25,617	23,733	24,266	20,597
Craftsmen, foremen, & kindred	11,082	10,435	9,465	9,241	8,205	8,350	6,203
Operative & kindred workers	14,335	13,406	12,254	12,846	11,754	12,030	9,518
Laborers, except farm & mine	3,751	3,515	3,755	3,530	3,774	3,885	4,875
Service workers	10,251	9,591	7,902	7,590	6,015	6,180	6,069
Private household workers	1,204	1,143	1,817	1,825	1,492	1,539	2,412
Service workers, exc. private	9,047	8,449	6,086	5,765	4,524	4,641	3,657
Farmworkers	**2,448**	**2,345**	**4,132**	**4,085**	**6,858**	**6,953**	**8,995**
Farmers & farm managers	1,428	1,350	2,528	2,526	4,325	4,375	5,362
Farm laborers & foremen	1,022	995	1,604	1,560	2,533	2,578	3,632

I searched for articles, popular and scholarly, about working class or poor Baby Boomers. I found nothing except for one study in a Special Edition of the 1974 *Journal of Social Issues,* volume 30, number 3, called "Youth, Generations and Social Change: Part II" edited by Vern L. Bengtson and Robert S. Loufer. In an article called "Generational Consciousness and Youth Movement Participation: Contrasts in Blue Collar and White Collar Youth," by

Patricia L. Kasschau, H. Edward Ransford, and Vern L. Bengtson, the authors show real differences among the values, attitudes, and actions of blue and white collar kids on college campuses. They also point out that blue collar Boomers not going to college exhibited an anti-authority and entitlement attitude because they were primarily responsible for increasing man hours lost due to labor strikes from 19 million in 1960, to over 42 million in 1968.

I called the distinguished Vern Bengtson at the Andrus School of Gerontology at the University of Southern California, and he sent me an extensive bibliography. None of the sources he sent directly spoke about Boomers from blue collar, poor, or small family-owned business backgrounds. I realized I was working in virgin intellectual territory. From a researcher's and former investigative reporter's point of view, this was very exciting stuff!

I asked my academic friends for help. Tom O'Connell is a long-time Boomer friend with whom I briefly lived communally in early 1970s. Tom's Ph.D. is in farmer and labor history, and he is a distinguished professor at Metropolitan State University in St. Paul, Minnesota. Tom had a real feel for my research because he teaches mostly older working adults (i.e., a lot of Boomers) returning to school for advanced degrees. He introduced me to Barbara Jensen who I mention extensively in Chapter 1 when I talk about the working class and the value of becoming. The two articles I used from Barbara are: "Belonging Versus Becoming: Psychology, Speech and Social Class," written in June, 1997 (unpublished), and "The Silent Psychology: A Presentation for the Youngstown Working Class Studies Conference" and published in the 1998 *Women's Studies Quarterly* (spring and summer issue).

I personally interviewed Barbara and read all of her published articles. She read a draft of *ReFirement*, Chapter 1, and gave an extensive telephone critique and review. Barbara is listed in the Resources section preceding these Chapter Notes.

The story of Sonny and his feelings about belonging as an African American came from a novel, *Losing Absalom* by Alexis D. Pate (Minneapolis: Coffee House Press, 1994).

My friend Tom O'Connell also introduced me to Peter Rachleff who is a labor historian, author, political activist, and chair of the

History Department at Macalester College in St. Paul, Minnesota. Peter told me about the list serve discussion going on among academics from working class backgrounds. He also introduced me to professor Elizabeth Higginbotham.

Elizabeth is identified in the section of Chapter 1 that talks about millions of Boomers of color growing up in poor neighborhoods. We had an extensive conversation and she sent me an article on upward mobility of African American women from middle class and poor economic backgrounds. The source for that article is "Moving Up with Kin and Community: Upward Social Mobility for Black and White Women" by Elizabeth Higginbotham and Lynn Weber found in the book, *Through the Prism Of Difference: Readings on Sex and Gender,* edited by Maxine Baca Zinn, Pierrette Hondagneu-Sotelo, and Michael A. Messner (Allyn and Bacon Press). Elizabeth stressed the value of giving back as one that is often shared across the poor and working class. She also read Chapter 1 for critique and review.

Elizabeth knows first-hand the pains and joys of growing up in an economically disadvantaged community. She particularly liked my distinction between poor and poverty. She also agreed the complex lives of young Boomers of color growing up in families where wages were very low has never really been fully explored or understood in White America.

The value of "risk taking" is one that I have learned from personal experience.

The values of "entitlement" and "expectations of the good life" came from *Rocking the Ages: The Yankelovich Report On Generational Marketing* by J. Walker Smith and Ann Clurman (New York: Harper Business Books, 1997). This book is also important for learning how to think from a generational perspective. As someone who has taught marketing at the graduate level and worked with many clients as a marketing consultant, I have been aware of the Yankelovich Partners since the early 1980s. They were the first firm to research, in depth, the attitudes of large buying and consuming groups in America based on common generational attitudes and experiences. Yankelovich has been doing this kind of marketing research profitably for over forty years. In this book, Smith and

Clurman discuss how many Boomers were raised permissively and believed they were something special. There are literally hundreds of articles in popular periodicals and scholarly journals about the psycho dynamics of Baby Boomers growing up in an unending era of prosperity. "Expectations of the good life" and "entitlement" are common Boomer descriptors—around long before *Rocking The Ages* was written.

ReFirement diverges from *Rocking the Ages* by trying to dig deeper and to understand the wide diversity of Boomers, as well as probing areas to see if there are things we all share in common across class, race, and gender. After reading *Rocking the Ages* and *ReFirement,* you will see that they both have similar perspectives common to anyone writing about Baby Boomers but they also have very different expressions.

The value of "experimentation" is so commonly connected to Boomers that it is hard to know where and when it was first officially reported.

In general, the most influential authors for me in advancing and deepening the generational and intergenerational thinking used in this chapter are William Strauss and Neil Howe who wrote *Generations: The History of America's Future 1584 to 2069* (New York: William Morrow, 1991). It is a must read for anyone who wants to seriously discuss ideas and concepts about different generations. I have cited them specifically when their ideas were used. I also relied on them for the quote from *Generations:* "Boomers built churches in the privacy of their own heads."

Strauss and Howe taught me that you can actually define a generation by common characteristics that emerge based on what influences a particular cohort during its youth. They also taught me to be aware of the myriad of influences that are around molding and shaping an entire generation. I learned that a generation is not just defined by some arbitrary years picked by demographers, but rather on how you define yourself in a generation based on your upbringing, values, and lifestyle. And finally, Strauss and Howe taught me that the generational characteristics are so strong, they tend to stick around for a long time after the generation that possessed them has passed into history.

Chapter 2: Turning Aging Upside Down

ESTHETIQUE is the very glossy magazine from Canada that is sent to dental and medical practices across the U.S. and the world. All of the information (including the ad copy cited in this chapter) about the size of the anti-aging, cosmetic enhancement industry, and the projected growth of that industry to one trillion dollars, came from the fall 1999 edition.

Web sites that support the information found in this chapter include the American Society For Dermatological Surgery (www.asds-net.org) and the American Society of Plastic and Reconstructive Surgeons, (www.plasticsurgery.org.) In fact, Paul Schnur M.D., the president of American Society for Plastic and Reconstructive Surgery, believes we will see a great rise in appearance enhancement therapies and treatments. Over two million people underwent aesthetic cosmetic surgery in 1999.

The figure of $100 billion we currently spend on cosmetic enhancements compared to the gross national products of Greece, Hungary, Denmark, and Austria and to the amounts given to private charities in the U.S., came from the *1998 World Atlas.* The figure on charitable giving includes individual and corporate contributions and not foundation grants. If you include foundation philanthropy, the total amount of money contributed in the U.S. in 1998 was about $195 billion.

Betty Friedan's book, *The Fountain of Age,* makes the argument that if Boomers accepted their own aging and aged maturely, it would cause a great economic and social upheaval in this country (see *ReFirement,* Resources, under Chapter 2).

All of the information on living intentionally intergenerationally came from eight years of extensive research and dialogues across the country and are referenced in my first book, *Together for Tomorrow: Building Community Through Intergenerational Dialogue* (see *ReFirement,* Resources, under Chapter 1).

My story on Harold and Robert came from Del Kennedy of the Union/Snyder Foster Grandparent Program in Sellingsgrove, Pennsylvania. For more information: acken@ptdprolog.net

The National Foster Grandparent's Conference took place in Orlando, Florida, in May 2000.

Chapter 3: Let's Retire Retirement!
The historical information about the retirement system came from Dora L. Costa's, *The Evolution of Retirement: An American Economic History (Chicago:* University of Chicago Press, 1998).

Eric Kingston and John Cornman made the comment about the real purpose of the retirement system—keeping certain workers out of the labor market—in an article called "Trends, Issues, Perspectives and Values for the Aging of the Baby Boom Cohorts," in *The Gerontologist* in February 1996.

I also used Nancy Dailey's seminal book, *When Baby Boomer Women Retire* (New York: Praeger Publishers, 1998), to document the history of retirement relating to people's productivity and age and the fact that retirement was never designed with women in mind. Dailey also makes a very strong case for the fact that we need to find a different paradigm for Boomer women as they reach traditional retirement age.

The statement that women receive only half the average pension that men receive came from *The Top Five Reasons Why Retirement is a Challenge to Women Workers,* published by the Wiser Women's Institute for a Secure Retirement in Washington D.C. Their Web site is: www.wiser.heinz/org/mainpage.html.

The *NBC Nightly News* lead story on January 1, 2000, reported the suicide and severe depression statistics cited in this chapter.

Page Smith is the retiree who wrote about retirement being "inhumane and probably immoral" in his book, *Old Age Is Another Country: A Traveler's Guide* (Freedom, California: Crossing Press, 1995).

The AARP cited information can be found in *AARP News,* July 1, 1999, under the title: "New AARP Survey Explores Differences In Boomer Attitudes About Retirement." Some interpretive information about the AARP survey was provided by Richard Chin in the St. Paul *Pioneer Press* article "Boomers Work To Redefine Retirement Survey Shows," June 3, 1998.

Chapter 4: Getting Your Groove Back
Daniel Okrent's quote came from the June 12, 2000 *Time* magazine article, "Twilight of the Boomers."

Victor Frankl's quote came from his book, *Man's Search for Meaning: From Deathcamp to Existentialism*. The full citation for *Flow* and *Man's Search for Meaning* is found in *ReFirement*, Resources, uner Chapter 4. Another good book for starting an optimal flow experience is *The Artist's Way* by Julia Cameron (New York: P. Putnam and Sons, 1995).

William Miller's book is *Your Golden Shadow: Discovering & Fulfilling Your Undeveloped Self* (San Francisco: Harper and Row, 1989).

Martin's story about his music came from *The Man Who Mistook His Wife For a Hat and Other Clinical Tales* by Oliver Sacks (New York: Harper and Row, 1987).

The Groucho Marks and Bernie Seigal quotes and information on humor and the immune system were taken from an article called "Health and Humor" by Paul E. McGhee, Ph.D. This article can be found at: www.holisticonline.com/humor-mcghee-article-htm

The Norman Cousins story was taken from an entertaining book called *Humor Is No Laughing Matter* by Mark Lee (Toronto Canada: Horizon House Publishers, 1981). If you wish to read Cousin's direct story, look for his article, "Anatomy of an Illness as Perceived by the Patient," in *The New England Journal of Medicine*, December 23, 1976.

The adventure story of Lyn was shared with me by my editor, Ron Klug, and his wife, Lyn.

Chapter 5: Taking Charge of Your Own Health

The information about the correlation between good health and education came from a report cited in *USA Today*, August 3, 2000. The same article emphasized how important it was for all of us to have access to positive social networks in order to maintain mastery and choices in our daily lives.

The research base for laughter and health benefits came from the McGhee article cited in Chapter 4 and *Don't Get Mad—Get Funny: A Light-Hearted Approach to Stress Management* by Leigh Anne Jasheway (Duluth, Minnesota: Whole Person Press, 1996).

The general information on staying healthy through preven-
tion came from many years of reading and my own prevention
regimen. I did use a couple of resources in writing this chapter and
they are: *Stretching For Fitness and Health Performance* by Dr.
Christopher A. Oswald and Dr. Stanley N. Bacso (New York: Sterling
Publishing Company, 1998); *Full Life Fitness: A Complete Exercise
Program for Mature Adults* by Janie Clark (Human Kinetics, 1992);
Walking For Health, Fitness and Sport by Bob Carlson (Fulcrum
Publications, 1996); *Strength Training Past 50* by Wayne Westcott
Ph.D. and Thomas R. Baechle, Ed.D. (Champaign, Illinois: Human
Kinetics, 1998); and *Between Heaven and Earth: A Guide To Chinese
Medicine* by Harriet Beinfield, L.Ac. and Efrem Korngold, L.Ac.,
O.M.D. (New York: Ballantine Books, 1991).

The *New England Journal of Medicine* citation on the number
of Americans using some form of alternative medical care is from
an article by David M. Eisenberg in Volume 328, 1993.

The Vilma Vitanza story came to me through Stu Kandell who
introduced me to Vilma. Stu is the Executive Director of
StAGEbridge Theater in San Francisco.

Chapter 6: Men Are from Mars. Women Are from Venus. But We Both Live on Earth!

The statistics on women have been widely reported by the major
news media. They are also documented in, Ernst & Young's
Financial Planning For Women (New York: John Wiley and Sons,
1999).

Nancy Dailey's book, *When Baby Boomer Women Retire,* cited
in Chapter Notes, Chapter 3 above, was used extensively in
Chapter 6 because she has completed, in my opinion, the most
comprehensive research and writing on Boomer women facing
retirement.

Information on male depression came from an article by Tracy
Thompson, in *Esquire,* December 1995.

The statistics on Boomer women as investors, heads of households, and doing better than men as investors came from "In-

Depth, NBC Special Report on Woman and Finances" on the *NBC Nightly News* during the week of February 14–18, 2000.

I also used the Women's Institute for a Secure Retirement (WISER) for background information. You can find WISER at www.wiser.heinz.org/mainpage.html

The Susan Faludi material was based on my interpretation of her book, *The Betrayal of the American Man* (New York: William Morrow and Company, 1999) and excerpted material in *Newsweek* magazine, September 13, 1999.

Chapter 7: Changing Through Healing and Forgiveness

The diversity figures for Boomers came from Eric Kingston and John Cornman in their article "Trends, Issues, Perspectives and Values for the Aging of the Baby Boom Cohorts," published in *The Gerontologist* in February 1996.

In the section of this chapter, Living In the Global Village, the material on the breakdown of the world's shrinking population came from the Mitsubishi Research Institute. The specific author is unknown. I do not agree with all of their findings especially about all of the world's wealthiest people living in the U.S. But the point of this information is to show how small the world really is. For more information contact the Institute at info@mri.co.jp

Chapter 8: Becoming an Elder-In-Training

The Barry Barkan quote and Reb Zalman's story of his continuing visits with his "inner elder" came from the book, *Age-ing to Sage-ing: A Profound New Vision Of Growing Older* by Zalman Schachter-Shalomi and Ronald Miller. More information about the book and the Age-ing to Sage-ing program is found in *ReFirement*, Resources section, under Chapter 8.

Ralph Nader's statement about Bill Gates can be found in his acceptance speech for the Green Party's nomination for president in 2000.

The Naisbitt information came from Leslie Miller's article in *USA Today*, October 28, 1999.

Chapter 9: What Really Spirits You?

The Jane Fonda story came from *O-The Oprah Magazine* and Oprah's interview with Jane in the July/August 2000 issue.

Cletus Wessels' statement came from his book, *The Holy Web* (Maryknoll, New York: Orbis, 2000.

Diarmuid O'Murchu's statement came from his book, *Our World in Transition: Making Sense of a Changing World* (Crossroad Classics, 2000).

Jean Morris Trumbauer helped me considerably in the early stages of this book with ideas and editorial direction. She was an inspiration for many of the ideas found in *ReFirement*. She also is an expert on spirituality. The information cited from Jean in this chapter and two of the ReFirement exercises came from her book, *Created and Called: Discovering Our Gifts For Abundant Living* (Minneapolis: Augsburg Fortress, 1998). Contact information can be found in *ReFirement*, Resources, under Chapter 9.

James Conlon's quotation came from his book, *Lyrics of Re-Creation* (New York: Continuum Publishing, 1997).

Victor Frankl's book *Man's Search For Meaning* is found in *ReFirement*, Resources, under Chapter 4.

Chapter 10: Developing Your Individual ReFirement Plan

The "simplicity of life" material is attributed to Joe and Vicki Robin from their best selling book, *Your Money or Your Life* (New York: Viking Penguin Books, 1992).

For a good example of how to really "mine your assets," look at the old standard, *What Color Is Your Parachute?* by Richard Nelson Bolles.

Richard Morgan is a personal friend of mine and an international authority on spirituality and aging. See *ReFirement*, Resources, under Chapter 9 for references and contact information.

Chapter 11: Claiming Your Legacy

For more information on the ethical will concept or to purchase an Ethical Will Resource Kit, see *ReFirement*, Resources, under Chapter 11.

Chapter 12: Building a ReFirement Movement
The information on the growth of the world wide web was taken from the *Graphic, Visualization & Useability Center's (GVU) 8th WWW User Survey.* All results are available on line at:
www.gvu.gatech.edu/user_surveys/survey-1997-10/#highsum

The quote from Robert Kennedy was found in the book, *The Baby Boomer Challenge* by Rev. Dr. Derald H. Edwards (Nashville: InterActive Resources, Inc., 1995).

www.ReFirement.org